Building a Career in AI: A Practical Guide for Aspiring Professionals

Jayant Deshmukh

Published by Jayant Deshmukh, 2024.

While every precaution has been taken in the preparation of this book, the publisher assumes no responsibility for errors or omissions, or for damages resulting from the use of the information contained herein.

BUILDING A CAREER IN AI: A PRACTICAL GUIDE FOR ASPIRING PROFESSIONALS

First edition. November 30, 2024.

Copyright © 2024 Jayant Deshmukh.

Written by Jayant Deshmukh.

Table of Contents

About the Author 1

Prologue 5

Introduction 9

Chapter 1: Understanding AI – More Than Just Buzzwords 15

Chapter 2: The AI Job Market 21

Chapter 3: Building the Foundation – Skills That Matter 33

Chapter 4: Learning AI – Roadmap for Beginners 39

Chapter 5: Gaining Experience – Projects That Stand Out 47

Chapter 6: The AI Professional's Toolkit 55

Chapter 7: Building a Personal Brand in AI 63

Chapter 8: Overcoming Challenges and Staying Motivated 71

Chapter 9: Landing Your First Job or Transitioning into AI 77

Chapter 10: Growing Your Career in AI 85

References 93

Conclusion 97

About the Author

Jayant Deshmukh is a seasoned professional with over 16 years of experience in project management, digital transformation, and technology innovation. A **Certified Project Management Professional (PMP)** and an accomplished **AI practitioner**, Jayant has worked with leading banks and financial institutions across the globe, spearheading digital transformation initiatives that have redefined industries and enhanced operational efficiency.

Having travelled extensively and worked in multiple countries, Jayant has gained a rich understanding of diverse geographies, cultures, and professional ecosystems. His experience with multinational corporations has provided him with deep insights into the unique challenges, aspirations, and personas of people from various walks of life. This global perspective has been instrumental in shaping his empathetic and solution-oriented approach to navigating technological and organizational complexities.

Beyond his professional accomplishments, Jayant is deeply committed to making a meaningful impact in the social sphere. He actively engages with communities, understanding the challenges faced by students, aspiring professionals, and mid-career individuals looking to pivot into artificial intelligence. This hands-on interaction fuels his passion for democratizing AI and helping individuals chart a clear, actionable path to success in this transformative field.

Jayant is also a prolific author, having penned several highly regarded books:

1. ***Prompt Engineering - The Ultimate Guide for Success in Artificial Intelligence***: A definitive guide to harnessing the power of AI through prompt engineering, offering practical tools and insights for beginners and professionals alike.
2. ***Mastering the Art of Corporate Communication***: A comprehensive exploration of 149 effective communication strategies in the corporate world, designed to enhance influence and collaboration.
3. ***Step by Step Guide to Overcome Corporate Politics***: A practical, storytelling-driven guide to navigating and resolving corporate politics, empowering readers to thrive in their professional journeys through 105 proven techniques.

In his latest book, *"Building a Career in AI: A Practical Guide for Aspiring Professionals"*, Jayant combines his technical expertise, leadership acumen, and human-centered perspective to create a roadmap for anyone looking to succeed in the field of AI. Whether you're a student exploring your future or a professional seeking to transition into AI, this book offers actionable steps, real-world examples, and motivational insights to guide your journey.

Jayant's unique blend of technical knowledge, cultural awareness, and commitment to empowering others makes his work both practical and inspiring. His writings are a testament to his belief that AI is not just a technology—it's a tool to unlock human potential and shape a better future for all.

Connect with Jayant Deshmukh on social media at :

https://www.instagram.com/jayantdeshmukhofficial/

https://www.linkedin.com/in/jayant-deshmukh-pmp/

https://www.facebook.com/jayantdeshmukh01

https://www.youtube.com/@jayantdeshm

https://www.threads.net/@jayantdeshmukhofficial

https://x.com/jayantdeshm

Prologue

In the quiet of November 2022, an unassuming event marked the dawn of a new era. OpenAI released ChatGPT, a tool so revolutionary that it shattered the barriers between humans and machines. For decades, artificial intelligence (AI) was a whisper on the wind—a vision of the future filled with both awe and skepticism. But with the launch of ChatGPT, that distant vision became an accessible reality, forever altering how we think, work, and live.

Before this breakthrough, AI was often perceived as an impossibility for the masses. Sure, it had made strides—autonomous cars, virtual assistants, and complex algorithms driving industries—but it remained an abstract concept for most people. Its intricate layers of machine learning, deep learning, and neural networks seemed the domain of elite experts. To the average individual, AI was a labyrinth too complex to navigate.

Then came ChatGPT.

With its conversational fluency and its ability to understand, generate, and engage, this AI wasn't just a technological marvel; it was a harbinger of change. Suddenly, AI wasn't about mysterious algorithms locked in research labs. It became something anyone could interact with—an ally in creativity, productivity, and innovation. Teachers used it to craft lesson plans, entrepreneurs to brainstorm ideas, students to learn, and professionals to automate routine tasks. ChatGPT turned the impossible into the achievable, democratizing AI in ways we hadn't imagined.

I still remember the moment I realized the profound impact of this transformation. I was speaking to a group of college students, brimming with curiosity about their futures. One of them asked, "Sir, how do I build a career in AI when I don't know where to start?" It struck a chord. These weren't just technical questions—they were the aspirations of a generation seeking to shape the future.

Later that day, I sat reflecting on my journey. Having spent years in the IT industry, orchestrating digital transformations and witnessing the rise of technologies, I had seen how AI was quietly becoming the backbone of industries. Yet, there was a glaring gap. AI was evolving rapidly, but the path to entering this field was unclear for many. The resources were scattered, the guidance fragmented, and for most people, AI still felt out of reach.

It was then that I decided to write this book.

I wanted to create something that bridged the gap—something that made AI accessible to anyone willing to learn, no matter their background or expertise. I wanted to demystify AI, turning it from an intimidating concept into an inspiring journey. And most importantly, I wanted to show people that their aspirations in AI are not just valid but achievable.

AI's story is one of persistence. In the 1950s, pioneers like Alan Turing and John McCarthy dreamt of machines that could think. But for decades, progress was slow, hindered by limited computational power and skepticism. It wasn't until the late 20th century that AI began to gather momentum, with neural networks, machine learning, and big data opening new doors.

Even then, AI was far from mainstream. The tools were complex, the infrastructure expensive, and the knowledge confined to specialists. The public saw glimpses—chess-playing computers, voice recognition software—but these were novelties, not necessities.

The real breakthrough came in the 2010s, with advancements in deep learning and cloud computing. AI began solving problems at scale, from diagnosing diseases to optimizing supply chains. Yet, it still felt like a technology reserved for corporations and researchers.

That changed with ChatGPT. In a single stroke, it showcased AI's potential for human interaction. It wasn't just solving problems; it was communicating, learning, and creating. It was the kind of innovation that rewrote the rules, making AI a part of daily life.

This book isn't just about AI. It's about you—your aspirations, your potential, and your ability to shape the future. It's for students dreaming of careers in cutting-edge fields, professionals seeking to transition into a world driven by AI, and anyone curious about the opportunities ahead.

I've structured this book not as a technical manual but as a guide, a mentor, and an inspiration. Through real-life stories, practical advice, and hands-on exercises, I want you to feel empowered. You don't need to be a tech genius or a programming prodigy to start. All you need is curiosity and the willingness to take the first step.

Let me share a story that encapsulates the spirit of this book. A few months after ChatGPT's launch, I met a school teacher named Meera. She'd always loved teaching but found herself struggling with the rapid shift to digital tools. AI seemed like a foreign land to her. "How can someone like me, with no technical background, make sense of this world?" she asked.

Together, we explored tools like ChatGPT, showing her how to use it to create lesson plans, personalize student feedback, and even brainstorm creative activities. Within weeks, Meera was not just comfortable with AI—she was thriving, using it to enhance her teaching in ways she'd never imagined.

Her journey was a testament to what's possible when curiosity meets opportunity. It's stories like Meera's that inspired me to write this book. Because for every Meera out there, there are countless others waiting to discover their potential in AI.

As you turn these pages, remember this: AI isn't the future—it's the present. The possibilities are endless, and the opportunities are waiting. You are standing at the edge of a revolution, one where your skills, creativity, and determination can shape industries and change lives.

Let this book be your guide, your companion, and your catalyst. Together, we'll explore the world of AI, not as something to fear, but as a tool to embrace. And as we embark on this journey, always keep in mind Franklin D. Roosevelt's wise words: **"The only limit to our realization of tomorrow will be our doubts of today."**

The path ahead is filled with promise. Let's walk it together.

Introduction

"The future belongs to those who prepare for it today." This quote by Malcolm X is particularly apt for this era, especially when it comes to artificial intelligence. As Andrew Ng puts it, **"AI is the new electricity."** Just as electricity transformed industries in the 20th century, AI is reshaping our world in ways we could only dream of a decade ago. This book is my humble attempt to be your guide as you embark on this exciting journey into AI—a field that promises to redefine careers, industries, and even our daily lives.

Why I Wrote This Book

Let me start by sharing a little about my own journey. I've spent over 16 years navigating the IT industry, working with global banks and financial institutions, and orchestrating digital transformations. During this time, I've seen firsthand how AI can turn challenges into opportunities. I've also observed the apprehension that many young students and professionals feel when faced with the complexity of AI.

One pivotal moment that inspired me to write this book came during a transition project I led for a major financial institution. AI wasn't just a tool; it was the very foundation of their transformation. Watching that project unfold, I realized the immense potential AI holds—not just for businesses, but for individuals aspiring to create meaningful careers.

I wrote this book to bridge the gap between aspiration and action, to demystify AI, and to provide a practical, step-by-step roadmap for anyone—whether you're a college student just starting out, or a seasoned professional looking to pivot into AI.

What This Book Contains

This book is designed to be more than just a guide—it's your companion on the journey to building a career in AI. Here's what you'll find:

1. **Foundations of AI**: We'll start with the basics, ensuring you understand what AI is and what it isn't.
2. **Career Paths**: Explore the diverse roles within the AI ecosystem—from data scientists to AI engineers—and find what suits you best.
3. **Skill Building**: Step-by-step guidance on the skills, tools, and resources you need to succeed.
4. **Real-Life Stories**: Learn from inspiring real-world examples of individuals who've built thriving careers in AI.
5. **Interactive Exercises**: Practical exercises to help you apply what you've learned and build confidence.
6. **Long-Term Growth**: Tips on staying relevant in a field that evolves at lightning speed.

How This Book Adds Value

AI is often seen as intimidating—a world filled with complex algorithms, endless jargon, and an ever-evolving landscape. My goal is to make this world accessible and relatable.

This book will:

- **Simplify the Complex**: Using clear explanations and storytelling, I'll break down the most complicated concepts into digestible insights.
- **Inspire Confidence**: Through relatable examples and actionable steps, you'll feel empowered to start your AI journey.
- **Offer Practical Guidance**: Whether it's learning Python,

building a portfolio, or acing an AI interview, you'll find concrete advice tailored to your needs.
- **Keep You Engaged**: The storytelling format ensures that learning feels less like a lecture and more like a conversation with a mentor.

The Impact of AI on Industries

Take a moment to think about how AI already impacts your life. The movie recommendations you enjoy on Netflix? AI. The traffic-free route suggested by Google Maps? AI. From healthcare diagnosing diseases to finance detecting fraud, AI is not just transforming industries; it's creating entirely new ones.

Consider this: By 2030, AI is expected to contribute $15.7 trillion to the global economy. Industries that were once slow to change—like agriculture, education, and even government—are now being revolutionized by AI. This unprecedented shift means an ever-growing demand for skilled AI professionals.

Who This Book Is For

This book is written for **two distinct groups** of readers:

1. **College Students and Young Professionals**
   If you're in college, wondering which career path to take, this book will help you understand why AI is one of the most promising choices today. It will guide you on where to start, how to learn, and how to stand out.
2. **Professionals Looking to Transition into AI**
   Perhaps you've been in the workforce for years and are now considering a career change. This book provides a clear roadmap for leveraging your existing skills and acquiring new ones to pivot into AI roles.

No matter which category you fall into, this book is for anyone willing to learn, adapt, and embrace the future.

One thing I've learned in my career is that stories resonate far more than statistics. That's why this book is crafted in a storytelling format. Each chapter includes real-life scenarios, relatable challenges, and practical solutions.

For example, you'll read about a college student who built an AI-powered chatbot as a class project and landed a dream job because of it. You'll also meet a mid-career professional who transitioned from IT operations to an AI-focused role, proving it's never too late to change paths.

By grounding concepts in real-world experiences, I aim to make learning not just informative but inspiring.

As you turn the pages of this book, you'll embark on a journey that's both exciting and transformative. You'll learn not only how to build a career in AI but also how to contribute meaningfully to a world that's increasingly driven by technology.

To end this introduction on an inspiring note:

***"The best way to predict the future is to invent it." –* Alan Kay**

The future belongs to AI—and it belongs to you. Let's get started.

"AI is not just the future of technology; it's the future of possibility."

— Jayant Deshmukh

Chapter 1: Understanding AI – More Than Just Buzzwords

It was a chilly winter morning, and Raj, a second-year computer science student, sat hunched over his laptop, staring at the code on the screen. For the past few weeks, he'd been working tirelessly on his college project—a simple chatbot for customer service. He had little idea then that this project, which started as an academic exercise, would be the turning point in his career. Raj's journey is not just an isolated story but one that mirrors what many students and professionals go through when they first encounter the world of Artificial Intelligence (AI).

At first glance, AI might sound like an elusive concept—a realm filled with jargon like machine learning, neural networks, deep learning, and data science. If you Google "AI," you'll likely come across a sea of confusing articles that either promise a utopia of self-driving cars or warn about an impending robot apocalypse. But what if I told you that AI is much more than buzzwords? It's already a part of your life, shaping your daily experiences, and this book will help you unlock the potential of AI, whether you're just starting out or looking to make a career change.

In this chapter, we'll break down AI, machine learning, and data science in simple terms. We'll explore how AI is quietly but powerfully impacting our lives and shaping the future. And we'll meet inspiring individuals—like Raj—who took a step into AI and transformed their careers in ways they never imagined.

What is AI?

Let's begin by defining AI.

Artificial Intelligence, or AI, is the simulation of human intelligence in machines. In simple terms, it's when a computer is designed to perform tasks that would typically require human brainpower—tasks like learning from experience, making decisions, or even recognizing patterns. It's not as complicated as it sounds. Think of AI as the brain behind various digital systems that can learn and adapt over time.

Now, you might be wondering: *How is AI different from regular computer programs?*

The difference is in how AI learns and improves itself. Traditional computer programs follow fixed instructions to perform specific tasks. They do exactly what they're told, no more, no less. But AI can learn from data, recognize patterns, and adapt its behavior without being explicitly programmed for every scenario.

For example, when you use Google Maps, it doesn't simply give you the same route every time. It learns from your previous searches, traffic data, and even real-time updates to recommend the best route. That's AI at work—constantly learning and evolving to improve user experience.

Machine Learning: The Heart of AI

Within the world of AI, there's a subset that's gaining more attention every day—Machine Learning (ML). Machine learning is a type of AI that allows systems to automatically learn and improve from experience, without being explicitly programmed.

Think about how Netflix recommends movies to you. The first time you open Netflix, it doesn't know much about you. But over time, it watches what genres you prefer, what movies you pause, and what shows you binge-watch in a weekend. Using this data, Netflix's AI system learns your preferences and suggests movies or series that it thinks you'll enjoy. The more you watch, the smarter it gets.

That's machine learning in action. It's about creating algorithms that can analyze vast amounts of data, find patterns, and make predictions based on those patterns. In Netflix's case, it's predicting which movie you'll want to watch next. In other cases, it might be predicting whether a loan applicant is likely to default on their loan based on their financial history.

But machine learning doesn't just analyze data; it improves itself over time. Think of it like a student who, after reading 100 books, can write an essay with more insights and depth than when they first started.

Data Science: The Backbone of AI

Now, let's talk about data science. Data science is the process of collecting, analyzing, and interpreting large volumes of data to uncover trends, patterns, and insights that can help inform decisions. You can think of data science as the toolbox used to build AI systems. Without data, AI wouldn't exist. It's data that feeds AI and helps it learn and evolve.

Imagine you are the owner of a retail store. You have thousands of customers purchasing items every day. The data from those transactions—like what items are being bought, when they're being bought, and by whom—can provide invaluable insights. Through data science, you could identify trends, such as the most popular items during the holiday season or patterns in customer buying behavior.

These insights can then be used to improve your business operations, from inventory management to targeted advertising. And the more data you gather, the better your AI-powered tools become at making predictions and recommendations.

AI in Everyday Life

By now, you might be thinking, *This sounds fascinating, but where do I actually see AI in my life?*

Let's take a look at how AI quietly powers many of the tools and services you already use.

1. **Google Maps:** When you open Google Maps, AI is working behind the scenes, analyzing data from millions of users to suggest the fastest routes, avoid traffic jams, and even predict how long it will take to get to your destination. It learns from historical data, real-time traffic updates, and your location to continuously improve the experience.
2. **Netflix Recommendations:** As mentioned earlier, Netflix uses AI to recommend movies based on your viewing history. But the real magic happens as you continue to watch. The more you engage with the platform, the more accurate and personalized the recommendations become.
3. **Voice Assistants (Siri, Alexa, Google Assistant):** These AI-powered assistants are designed to understand human language, answer questions, set reminders, and even control your smart home devices. They learn from your voice, understand your preferences, and can anticipate your needs.
4. **Spam Filters:** If you've ever used email, you've likely seen a spam folder. But how does your email provider know which messages are spam and which are important? AI. It uses machine learning algorithms to detect patterns in emails—like suspicious subject lines, unfamiliar senders, and certain keywords—and filters out spam messages accordingly.
5. **Self-Driving Cars:** While still in the early stages, self-driving cars are perhaps the most iconic example of AI in action. These cars use sensors, machine learning, and real-time data to navigate streets, avoid obstacles, and make decisions on the road.

These are just a few examples, but AI is everywhere. It's in the devices you use, the apps you interact with, and the services you rely on.

The Inspiring Story of Raj: Turning a College Project into a Career in AI

Let me share the story of Raj, a student much like you. Raj had always been fascinated by technology. But AI? That was a whole different world. In his second year of college, he chose a project to build a chatbot for customer service—something simple but effective. He had no idea that this project would be the beginning of his journey into the AI industry.

At first, Raj struggled. He wasn't sure how to make his bot understand natural language. He spent countless hours coding, tweaking, and testing. But rather than giving up, Raj took a step back and decided to learn from the vast array of AI resources available online. He enrolled in a few free online courses and read everything he could about machine learning.

Fast forward a few months, and Raj's chatbot was able to answer customer queries with remarkable accuracy. The project caught the attention of his professors, and soon enough, it caught the eye of a tech startup. They were looking for a fresh talent with experience in AI, and Raj's project became his gateway into a full-time AI engineering role.

What's more inspiring is that Raj didn't come from an AI background. He was just a student, curious and willing to learn. Today, he works as a machine learning engineer at a leading tech company, using the very skills he built during his college project to solve real-world problems. Raj's story proves that with determination, the right resources, and a bit of curiosity, anyone can transition into the field of AI.

Conclusion: The New Electricity

As Andrew Ng wisely said, *"AI is the new electricity."* Just as electricity changed the world in the early 20th century, AI is now shaping our present and future. It's no longer a distant dream or something reserved for tech giants; AI is here, and it's changing the world in ways we never imagined.

Whether you're a student, a professional, or just someone curious about the future, AI offers endless possibilities. And the best part? It's accessible to anyone willing to learn. You don't need to be a genius or a tech prodigy. What you need is curiosity, the willingness to put in the work, and the drive to explore this exciting new world.

Let Raj's story be a reminder that AI is for anyone—no matter where you're starting from. And as you continue reading this book, you'll realize that you, too, can build a career in AI, harnessing its potential to create a better, smarter world.

Now that you understand the basics of AI, machine learning, and data science, let's move on to exploring how these fields will shape your future career. Stay with me; the journey is just beginning.

Chapter 2: The AI Job Market

As the sun set over the bustling city of Bengaluru, Aarav sat at his desk, staring at the job postings on his screen. He had recently graduated with a degree in computer science, and while his classmates were already working in traditional IT roles, Aarav had his eyes set on something different. He was drawn to the world of AI, a field that seemed to hold limitless possibilities. But despite the excitement, a sense of uncertainty lingered. The world of AI was vast, and Aarav wasn't sure where to start.

As he scrolled through job descriptions, he noticed a wide array of roles: **Data Scientist, AI Engineer, Machine Learning Researcher, AI Product Manager**, and many more. The titles were unfamiliar and the requirements daunting. Aarav felt a twinge of doubt. Was AI only for the elite few who had years of experience or were scholars of deep mathematics and algorithms? Was there a place for someone like him, who had a basic understanding of AI but wasn't an expert?

Aarav wasn't alone in his confusion. Many young professionals and students, like you, are at a similar crossroads when they consider a career in AI. On one hand, the industry is booming, with a wide array of opportunities. On the other hand, there seems to be a vast gap between the demand for AI talent and the skills available in the job market. But let me tell you this—**this is your moment.**

In this chapter, we will explore the dynamic and rapidly evolving AI job market, dive into the roles that are shaping the future, look at how industries like healthcare and finance are being transformed by AI, and analyze the global demand for AI professionals. More importantly, we'll also discuss why now is the best time to build a career in AI.

AI Roles: More Than Just Titles

When we think of AI jobs, the first thing that often comes to mind are the roles of **Data Scientist** or **AI Engineer**. But the world of AI is much more expansive than that, offering a range of exciting and impactful positions. Let's break down some of the most sought-after roles and what they entail.

1. **Data Scientist**:
   A data scientist is often seen as the "rock star" of the AI world. The role involves analyzing complex data to find patterns, make predictions, and help organizations make data-driven decisions. But it's not just about numbers and algorithms. A data scientist needs a blend of technical and business acumen. They must understand not only how to extract meaningful insights from data but also how those insights can solve real-world business problems.

Aarav, for example, could become a data scientist if he were comfortable with programming languages like Python and R, statistical analysis, and data visualization tools. This role requires a deep understanding of machine learning algorithms and the ability to apply them to business needs. A strong foundation in mathematics, particularly linear algebra and probability, is often necessary.

1. **AI Engineer**:
   AI engineers focus on designing, building, and deploying AI models. They work closely with data scientists to implement machine learning algorithms into real-world applications. While data scientists often focus on the research and theoretical aspects of AI, AI engineers take those theories and turn them into tangible, working solutions.

If Aarav were to pursue a career as an AI engineer, he would need proficiency in programming languages like Python, Java, and C++. A solid understanding of cloud computing platforms such as AWS or Azure is also crucial, as many AI models are deployed on the cloud. Unlike data scientists, AI engineers work more closely with infrastructure and architecture, ensuring that AI solutions can scale efficiently.

1. **Machine Learning Researcher**:
   Machine learning researchers are the pioneers, pushing the boundaries of AI by developing new algorithms and refining existing ones. This role is more research-oriented and requires a deep understanding of computer science and mathematics. Machine learning researchers often work in academic or corporate research labs, publishing papers and collaborating with other experts in the field.

Aarav could aim for this role if he's particularly interested in advancing the field of AI. It requires a strong academic background, often at the master's or Ph.D. level, and a passion for innovation. Machine learning researchers usually specialize in specific areas of AI, such as natural language processing (NLP), computer vision, or reinforcement learning.

1. **AI Product Manager**:
   AI product managers combine technical expertise with business strategy. They work closely with engineers and data scientists to develop AI products and services that align with business goals. Unlike traditional product managers, AI product managers must have a solid understanding of AI technologies and how to apply them in product development.

This role is a great fit for someone like Aarav if he has a keen interest in both technology and business. While he might not be directly building AI models, he would need to understand how AI can be leveraged to create innovative products. A deep understanding of market needs, user experience, and how AI can solve real-world problems is essential.

1. **AI Consultant:**

   As more companies look to implement AI, there is a growing demand for consultants who can guide organizations through the process. AI consultants help businesses identify opportunities where AI can add value, implement AI solutions, and measure their effectiveness. This role requires a mix of technical knowledge, business strategy, and communication skills.

For someone like Aarav who enjoys working with different organizations and solving complex problems, becoming an AI consultant could be an ideal career path. It involves working with diverse teams across industries, helping them integrate AI into their operations, and ensuring that AI solutions are aligned with business goals.

These are just a few examples of the many roles available in the AI field. The good news is that the demand for these positions is growing exponentially, and they span across almost every industry. Whether you're a technical person or someone with a business mindset, there's an AI role for you.

Case Study: The Transformation of Healthcare and Finance Through AI

AI is transforming industries, and few sectors have been as profoundly impacted as healthcare and finance. Let's take a look at how these industries are being reshaped by AI.

1. **AI in Healthcare:**

   Healthcare has traditionally been slow to adopt new

technologies, but AI is changing that. AI applications in healthcare range from predictive analytics to personalized medicine, and everything in between. For example, AI is being used to analyze medical images and assist doctors in diagnosing diseases such as cancer and tuberculosis. Machine learning models are trained on vast datasets of medical images to detect patterns that might be missed by the human eye. This has the potential to save lives and improve patient outcomes.

AI is also revolutionizing personalized medicine. Algorithms are being developed to analyze an individual's genetic makeup, lifestyle, and medical history to create personalized treatment plans. Imagine a world where your doctor doesn't just prescribe generic treatments but tailors every prescription to your unique health profile. AI is making this a reality.

Aarav, had he chosen to enter the healthcare AI field, might have worked on developing these predictive models, helping save lives with the same technology he used in his college chatbot project. The opportunities for AI in healthcare are boundless, and as the industry continues to embrace AI, it will need more talented professionals to drive innovation.

1. **AI in Finance**:
   In finance, AI is reshaping everything from fraud detection to trading algorithms. AI systems are used to detect patterns of fraudulent activity by analyzing transaction data in real-time. By examining millions of transactions, AI can spot anomalies that might indicate fraud, preventing financial losses.

AI is also used in algorithmic trading, where machines make decisions to buy and sell stocks based on market data. These AI systems can analyze massive amounts of information in seconds and make trades that would take a human trader much longer.

For someone like Aarav with a solid foundation in machine learning, working in AI for finance could involve building fraud detection systems, analyzing financial markets, or developing AI-driven tools for personal finance. The financial industry is one of the largest employers of AI talent, and the demand for professionals with AI skills is skyrocketing.

Expanding the Horizons: More Personas Making the Transition

While Aarav's story exemplifies someone with a technical background, it's important to understand that AI is a field that is evolving so rapidly that it is accessible to people from all walks of life—even those with no prior experience in technology. AI is not just for mathematicians, data scientists, or engineers anymore. Let me introduce you to a few more personas—individuals from diverse fields who, just like Aarav, took a leap into the AI world and are now thriving.

Persona 1: Priya – From Marketing to Data Science

Priya was always the life of the party in her marketing team. She had a flair for creative campaigns, was adept at understanding consumer behavior, and had a deep passion for storytelling. However, after spending a few years working with digital marketing analytics, she realized there was something missing—she wanted to dive deeper into data, make data-driven decisions, and understand the "why" behind consumer trends. Priya's curiosity led her to AI.

At first, Priya felt intimidated. As someone who had never worked with complex algorithms, the world of machine learning and data science felt like a foreign language. But she was determined. She began by learning basic Python and enrolled in an online course about AI for business professionals. The course was tailored to help non-technical professionals like Priya grasp the fundamentals without getting lost in complex code.

Priya started to experiment with simple machine learning models to predict consumer behavior based on previous campaigns. She discovered the power of predictive analytics: by analyzing consumer purchase history, demographic data, and browsing patterns, she could now make far more accurate predictions about what customers were likely to buy next. Priya then used these insights to optimize her marketing strategies.

Today, Priya works as a **Data Scientist** for a global e-commerce company. She continues to apply her marketing expertise, but now she uses AI models to create highly personalized marketing campaigns, optimizing conversion rates and customer loyalty. Priya's story shows that if you come from a field where data is already integral to your work, transitioning to AI is not just possible—it's a huge advantage.

Persona 2: Ramesh – From Finance to AI Product Management

Ramesh had spent over a decade working as a senior financial analyst at a major bank. His role was heavily focused on analyzing stock trends, managing portfolios, and providing recommendations for investment strategies. Despite his success, he had become disillusioned with the static nature of his job. He longed to work in a field that was dynamic and on the cutting edge of technology. Ramesh had always been curious about AI, but he didn't know where to start.

One day, while attending a finance seminar, Ramesh learned about AI's growing influence on the financial industry—specifically, its ability to predict stock market trends, detect fraud, and optimize investment strategies. He was fascinated. Ramesh realized that AI could provide the perfect combination of his analytical skills and his desire to be part of something transformative.

He decided to take the plunge. Ramesh started by taking a few courses on AI fundamentals and product management. The idea of **AI Product Management** particularly intrigued him because it combined his experience in finance with a new challenge in AI development. Ramesh began to focus on understanding the lifecycle of AI products, from ideation to deployment, and how AI technologies could be used to solve problems in finance.

Within a year, Ramesh transitioned to an AI-focused product management role at a tech company that was developing fraud detection algorithms for banks. His deep understanding of financial systems gave him a unique advantage in creating AI-driven products that could revolutionize the way banks detect fraudulent activities. Today, he leads a team working on AI solutions that are changing the way the banking sector operates.

Ramesh's experience illustrates how professionals with strong business and industry knowledge can transition into AI roles without a technical background. In his case, he combined his financial expertise with AI product management to become a leader in a rapidly growing field.

Persona 3: Anjali – From Education to AI for Social Good

Anjali, a teacher with a master's degree in social sciences, always felt passionate about using education to uplift disadvantaged communities. She had worked in rural areas for years, helping young students learn, but she always felt that there was a limit to what traditional education systems could do. When she heard about the potential for AI to bring about social change, she was intrigued. She had never imagined that someone from her background could contribute to this field.

Despite her lack of technical experience, Anjali dove into the world of AI through MOOCs (Massive Open Online Courses), initially focusing on **AI for Social Good**. She began to understand how AI could address complex societal challenges such as access to education, healthcare, and poverty alleviation. She started volunteering for NGOs and social enterprises that were leveraging AI to develop affordable learning solutions for marginalized children.

Anjali's breakthrough came when she helped design an AI-powered platform that personalized learning for students based on their abilities. The platform could adapt to each student's unique learning style and pace, something that was particularly useful for children in remote areas with limited resources. Anjali worked closely with data scientists and engineers to ensure that the AI system was designed in a way that could be used in low-bandwidth environments.

Her success was a result of combining her passion for education with the growing potential of AI. Today, Anjali is an **AI Specialist** for an international non-profit organization, designing AI solutions that are transforming education systems in underserved communities across the world.

Anjali's story is proof that AI is not just for engineers and coders. It's a tool that anyone with a passion for solving real-world problems can use to make a significant impact. Whether your expertise lies in education, healthcare, or another field, AI has a place for you.

Global Demand vs. The Skills Gap: Why This is Your Moment

The demand for AI professionals is outpacing the supply, creating a significant skills gap. According to reports, by 2030, AI could add as much as $15 trillion to the global economy, but to tap into that potential, there's a critical need for skilled workers.

As the world grapples with AI's rapid expansion, one thing is clear: there is a massive **skills gap**. In 2020, a report from the World Economic Forum found that while demand for AI professionals was surging, there were not enough trained individuals to meet that demand. And this gap continues to widen. Today, there are millions of AI-related job openings across the globe, yet there is a shortage of qualified professionals to fill them.

But this is where you come in. Whether you're like Aarav, with a technical background, or like Priya, Ramesh, and Anjali, coming from fields like marketing, finance, or education, the time is ripe for anyone with a willingness to learn to step into the world of AI. There are countless opportunities for you to create a meaningful career in this space. From AI product management to social good, from healthcare to finance, industries are actively seeking professionals who can bridge the gap between business and technology.

AI is the future, and this is your moment to be part of that future. The demand for AI talent has never been greater, and the opportunity to build a career in AI has never been more accessible. The skills gap is real, but it's also your opportunity to fill it and shape the future.

The Best Way to Predict the Future Is to Invent It

As Alan Kay once said, **"The best way to predict the future is to invent it."** The future of AI is not set in stone—it's being written by people like you. Whether you're a student like Aarav, or someone looking to pivot into AI from another field like Priya, Ramesh, or Anjali, your journey starts here. Whether you choose to become a data scientist, AI engineer, or AI product manager, you are stepping into a world of endless possibilities.

This is your moment. The AI job market is full of opportunities, and as long as you're willing to learn and adapt, you'll be ready to seize them. In the next chapters, we'll dive deeper into how you can develop the skills needed to succeed in this exciting field, whether you're just starting or looking to take your career to the next level.

The world is waiting for innovators like you.

Chapter 3: Building the Foundation – Skills That Matter

When we talk about AI, we often think about groundbreaking innovations like self-driving cars, voice assistants, or personalized recommendations on streaming platforms. But behind all these marvels lies something simple yet profound: the foundation. Just like how a skyscraper stands tall on a well-constructed base, your career in AI requires you to start with solid foundational skills. These skills, though often overlooked, are the building blocks of your AI journey. In this chapter, we will explore the essential skills you need to build a career in AI and how to acquire them, whether you're just starting out or looking to deepen your expertise.

As Benjamin Franklin wisely said, *"An investment in knowledge pays the best interest."* Your journey in AI is an investment, and the more you invest in building your skills, the higher your return will be. So, let's dive into these crucial skills—mathematics, programming, and domain knowledge—and understand how each of them will play a pivotal role in your AI career.

Core Skills: The Pillars of AI

Mathematics: The Language of AI

For many, the word "mathematics" can sound intimidating. But in AI, math is not just a subject from school; it's the very language that allows computers to learn, predict, and make decisions. If you've ever wondered how AI systems can predict your next movie based on your viewing history or recommend products you might like, it all boils down to mathematical principles—especially linear algebra, calculus, probability, and statistics.

Take a moment and think about how you use maps every day. Let's say you're using **Google Maps** to find the quickest route to a friend's house. Behind the scenes, Google Maps uses algorithms that are powered by mathematical concepts like graph theory, which helps find the shortest path. This is just one example of how math powers many AI systems that we use in our daily lives.

Don't let the complexity of these mathematical concepts discourage you. Understanding the fundamentals will give you the ability to grasp how AI algorithms work and how to tweak them for real-world applications. You don't need to be a genius mathematician, but a solid understanding of concepts like **linear algebra** (which deals with vectors and matrices) and **probability** (which helps machines make predictions) will be incredibly valuable as you progress.

Programming: Turning Ideas into Reality

Now, let's talk about **programming**, the second critical skill. Without programming, AI remains just an abstract idea. Programming is the tool that allows you to bring your AI models to life. If math is the language of AI, programming is the medium through which it speaks.

The most widely used programming language in AI is **Python**. If you've heard about Python and are thinking it sounds like another snake in the wild, don't worry—you're not alone! When I first heard about it, I wasn't sure what the buzz was about. But once I started learning Python, I realized why it's the go-to language for AI professionals. It's simple, readable, and versatile. Python has libraries like **NumPy**, **Pandas**, **TensorFlow**, and **Scikit-learn** that make it easy to manipulate data, create machine learning models, and experiment with AI algorithms.

Let me share a story about **Rajesh**, a self-taught programmer who turned his basic Python skills into a thriving AI career. Rajesh had always been interested in computers and programming, but he worked in a non-technical role at a logistics company. One day, his team faced a problem: it took too long to process large amounts of data, and as a result, the company wasn't able to provide timely solutions to clients.

Rajesh decided to take action. He started by learning Python through online tutorials. At first, it felt like a steep learning curve, but Rajesh stuck with it. He learned the basics—variables, loops, and functions—then moved on to more advanced concepts like object-oriented programming and working with APIs. Slowly, he started applying these skills to the problems he faced at work.

One day, Rajesh wrote a Python script that automated the data-processing task, reducing the time it took to process client requests by 75%. This small success sparked something in Rajesh. He realized that AI wasn't just for tech companies—it could be applied in any industry to solve real-world problems.

This success led Rajesh to delve deeper into AI. He learned about machine learning, explored libraries like **TensorFlow** and **PyTorch**, and worked on projects that involved predictive analytics and classification models. Rajesh is now an **AI Engineer** at a leading tech firm, where he develops cutting-edge machine learning models for business solutions.

Rajesh's story is proof that you don't need to be an expert programmer from the start. With a basic understanding of Python and a willingness to learn, anyone can step into the world of AI and start making a difference.

Domain Knowledge: The Secret Sauce

While mathematics and programming are essential to understanding AI, **domain knowledge** is what separates the good from the great. Domain knowledge refers to your understanding of a specific industry or area—such as healthcare, finance, or marketing—where AI can be applied to solve real-world problems.

Consider **Anjali**, a former healthcare professional who made a career transition into AI. Anjali had been working as a nurse for over a decade, but when she saw how AI was transforming the healthcare industry, she decided to pivot. She had always been interested in technology, but without a technical background, she wasn't sure how to get started.

Anjali took a unique approach: she combined her healthcare expertise with AI. She enrolled in online AI courses and learned the basics of machine learning. But instead of applying her skills generically, she focused on how AI could improve patient care, optimize hospital operations, and predict disease outbreaks. Anjali worked on projects involving predictive analytics for patient monitoring and AI-powered diagnostic tools.

Today, Anjali is an **AI Researcher** specializing in healthcare AI, where she develops models that help doctors diagnose diseases more accurately and improve patient outcomes. Her deep domain knowledge gave her an edge in the AI field, and she now uses her expertise to create solutions that make a meaningful impact on people's lives.

In AI, domain knowledge allows you to focus your technical skills on solving problems that matter. Whether you're interested in **AI for finance**, **AI for education**, or **AI for sustainability**, your understanding of a particular industry will guide how you apply AI to solve challenges specific to that field.

Learning Paths: How to Build These Skills

For Beginners

If you're just starting your AI journey, it might feel overwhelming, but it doesn't have to be. The key is to take small, manageable steps.

1. **Start with the Basics**: Begin by learning foundational skills like Python programming and math. There are plenty of free resources and courses available to help you get started. Websites like **Coursera**, **edX**, and **Kaggle** offer introductory courses in Python and machine learning that cater to beginners.
2. **Pick Your Path**: AI is a vast field, so it's important to narrow your focus. You can choose to specialize in areas like **machine learning**, **natural language processing (NLP)**, or **computer vision**. Start with an area that excites you and dive deeper.
3. **Work on Projects**: Apply what you've learned by working on personal or open-source projects. This hands-on experience will solidify your understanding and make you more confident in your skills.
4. **Join a Community**: The AI community is vast and welcoming. Join forums, attend meetups, and connect with professionals who share your interests. Platforms like **GitHub**, **Reddit**, and **LinkedIn** are great places to start.

For Professionals Looking to Transition

If you already have some technical expertise and are looking to transition into AI, focus on the following:

1. **Leverage Your Existing Skills**: If you're coming from a field like software engineering, data analysis, or even marketing, you likely already have transferable skills. Build upon your existing knowledge and learn how to apply it in AI contexts.
2. **Advanced Courses and Specializations**: Once you have a basic understanding of AI, move on to more advanced topics

such as deep learning, reinforcement learning, and AI ethics. Platforms like **DeepLearning.ai** offer specialized courses on deep learning, while **Stanford University** and **MIT** offer in-depth resources on machine learning and AI.

3. **Collaborate on Projects**: Work with others on AI-focused projects to gain experience and insights into real-world applications of AI. Whether it's through your current job or as part of a side project, collaboration is key to learning.

Conclusion: Building a Strong Foundation for Your AI Career

Just like any great endeavor, building a career in AI requires a solid foundation. By developing key skills in mathematics, programming, and domain knowledge, you're not just preparing yourself for a job—you're preparing yourself to be a leader in a field that will define the future.

Remember, as **Benjamin Franklin** said, "**An investment in knowledge pays the best interest.**" The more you invest in yourself and your skills, the greater the rewards will be.

Whether you're just starting or looking to pivot your career, the journey into AI is one of continual learning. But with the right mindset and the right foundation, you'll be well on your way to becoming a future leader in AI.

The world of AI is waiting for innovators like you.

Chapter 4: Learning AI – Roadmap for Beginners

When I first ventured into the world of AI, the landscape was vastly different from what it is today. The field was still in its early stages of exploration, with only a few scattered resources available to the public. Fast forward to today, and the explosion of online learning platforms, tutorials, and free courses has made learning AI more accessible than ever before. The key to entering the world of AI is not just about acquiring knowledge—it's about applying that knowledge and showing that you can make a tangible impact. In this chapter, we'll dive into how you can start learning AI, build a portfolio, and take actionable steps to land a job in the field.

Let me take a moment to share one of my own experiences. Early in my career, I took a deep dive into the world of AI, but the resources back then were limited. Fast forward to today, and I see aspiring professionals armed with an arsenal of resources that can help them on their way. The availability of online courses, communities, and platforms has dramatically shifted the AI learning curve. For anyone starting today, the road to becoming an AI professional is clearer and more structured than ever before.

1. Resources: Where to Start Your AI Journey

When you're new to AI, the sheer volume of resources available can be overwhelming. You might wonder, **Where do I even begin? Which course should I take?** The answer depends on your learning style, but I'll break it down into a few key recommendations: **online courses, books, and certifications**.

Online Courses: The Fast Track to AI

One of the most effective ways to learn AI today is through **online platforms**. These platforms offer structured, beginner-friendly courses that break down complex topics into manageable chunks. Here are a few of the best resources I've personally found valuable:

- **Coursera**: This platform offers high-quality courses from top universities like Stanford, MIT, and Google. If you're a beginner, I highly recommend starting with **Andrew Ng's Machine Learning Course**. It's widely considered the gold standard for new learners. The course covers everything from the basics of machine learning to more complex topics like linear regression and neural networks.

Another excellent course is **DeepLearning.ai's Deep Learning Specialization**, which will take you through the fundamentals of deep learning and introduce you to advanced topics like convolutional neural networks (CNNs) and recurrent neural networks (RNNs). I can't emphasize enough how these foundational courses helped me get a foothold in AI.

- **edX**: Another platform with excellent beginner courses is **edX**. They offer courses from institutions like Harvard, MIT, and Microsoft. If you're just starting, I suggest looking at **Harvard's Data Science Professional Certificate**. It's an introductory series of courses designed to build your understanding of data science, which is closely linked to AI.
- **Kaggle**: If you're someone who learns best by doing, **Kaggle** is a platform you'll want to explore. It's one of the best places to practice machine learning, work with real datasets, and even compete in AI challenges. Kaggle offers tutorials on everything from Python programming to deep learning, and you'll find datasets from different domains—finance, healthcare, and sports, to name a few—that will help you

develop hands-on experience.
- **Fast.ai**: If you're keen to dive into deep learning, **Fast.ai** is another fantastic resource. What sets Fast.ai apart is that it's built for learners who already have a basic understanding of programming. The course is incredibly hands-on, with a focus on using cutting-edge libraries like **PyTorch**. The community around Fast.ai is also very active, which means you can connect with fellow learners and seek help when needed.

Books: The Roadmap to Deeper Understanding

While online courses offer quick, practical knowledge, books can give you a deeper, more nuanced understanding of AI. Some of the books I recommend for beginners are:

- **"Artificial Intelligence: A Modern Approach" by Stuart Russell and Peter Norvig**: This is often considered the "bible" for AI. It's comprehensive, well-structured, and has been used by thousands of AI professionals to get a deep understanding of the principles behind AI. Though it's quite technical, it's an invaluable resource as you get more comfortable with the field.
- **"Python Machine Learning" by Sebastian Raschka**: Once you've got your footing in Python, this book will help you dive into machine learning. It covers a wide array of topics, from data preprocessing to more advanced machine learning techniques like deep learning and model optimization.
- **"Hands-On Machine Learning with Scikit-Learn, Keras, and TensorFlow" by Aurélien Géron**: This book is an excellent choice if you're keen on getting your hands dirty with code. It's full of practical exercises that teach machine learning using Python and some of the most popular libraries in the AI space.

Certifications: Adding Credibility to Your Resume

While skills and hands-on projects are the most important factors for landing a job in AI, certifications can be a valuable way to show potential employers that you've dedicated time and effort to mastering a particular area. Some highly regarded AI certifications include:

- **Google AI's TensorFlow Developer Certification**: TensorFlow is one of the most widely used machine learning frameworks, and being certified in it can help you stand out in the job market. Google's certification program is a great way to get hands-on experience with deep learning and neural networks.
- **IBM Data Science Professional Certificate**: This is another great certification for beginners. It covers Python, SQL, data analysis, and machine learning, providing a strong foundation in data science, which is closely intertwined with AI.
- **Microsoft Certified: Azure AI Engineer Associate**: If you're interested in cloud computing and how it integrates with AI, this certification from Microsoft could be a great addition to your portfolio.

2. Building a Portfolio – The Importance of Hands-On Projects

As you start building your AI skills, there's one crucial thing that will differentiate you from the rest: a **portfolio**. A portfolio is a collection of real-world projects you've worked on, and it's one of the best ways to showcase your capabilities to potential employers. Simply having certificates on your resume is no longer enough—you need to prove that you can solve real problems using AI.

The Power of Hands-On Projects

To be successful in AI, you need to move beyond theory and get your hands dirty with practical, real-world applications. The more projects you can add to your portfolio, the better.

Let me share the story of **Nina**, a recent college graduate who used online courses and Kaggle to land her first AI job. Nina was studying economics when she developed an interest in AI. She started by taking Andrew Ng's **Machine Learning course** on Coursera, and though the theory was intriguing, she felt like she needed to apply her knowledge to something practical.

So, Nina began participating in Kaggle competitions, applying machine learning algorithms to datasets she found on the platform. One of her first projects involved predicting house prices based on various features like location, square footage, and amenities. Nina built a machine learning model that outperformed the baseline model by 20%, and she posted her code on GitHub.

This hands-on experience was a game-changer for Nina. When she started applying for AI jobs, she could point to specific projects she had worked on and demonstrate her skills to potential employers. Her portfolio became the centerpiece of her resume, and she quickly landed a position as a **Machine Learning Engineer** at a major tech company.

Tips for Building Your Portfolio

Here are some tips for creating an impressive portfolio:

- **Focus on Solving Real Problems**: Build projects that address real-world problems. It could be anything from predicting stock prices to classifying images. The goal is to show that you can apply AI to solve meaningful challenges.
- **Use Public Datasets**: Platforms like **Kaggle**, **UCI Machine Learning Repository**, and **Google Dataset Search** provide

free access to datasets that you can use for your projects.
- **Make Your Work Accessible**: Host your projects on **GitHub** and write detailed explanations in your project README files. This will help potential employers understand your thought process and the methodologies you've used.
- **Get Feedback**: Share your projects with the AI community on **Reddit, LinkedIn**, or **GitHub**. Constructive feedback will help you improve your work and build a strong reputation.

3. Real-Life Example – The Power of Persistence

I'd like to share the story of **Ravi**, a young college graduate with no prior experience in AI but a burning passion for technology. Ravi was initially intimidated by AI. He didn't have a technical background—he was a business major—but he had always been interested in how AI was reshaping the world.

Ravi began by following a learning path: he took **Andrew Ng's Machine Learning course**, then tackled Python programming, and slowly started building projects. His breakthrough came when he joined Kaggle. Ravi worked on a **predictive analytics** project using a healthcare dataset, which involved predicting patient outcomes based on historical data. Though it took him a few weeks to get the model right, he was determined.

He posted his results on Kaggle, showcasing the accuracy improvements and even explained his approach in a blog post. His work caught the attention of a recruiter from a major healthcare firm. Ravi landed an interview and was offered his first **AI Analyst** role, all thanks to his persistence and his Kaggle project.

4. Interactive Exercise – Your Learning Plan for the Next 6 Months

Now that you've seen what works for others, it's time to create a learning plan tailored to your goals. Here's an exercise to outline your roadmap for the next six months.

Month 1-2: Build foundational knowledge.

- Take **Andrew Ng's Machine Learning Course**.
- Learn the basics of Python if you're not already familiar with it. Resources like **Codecademy** and **Python.org** can help.

Month 3-4: Start hands-on projects.

- Choose a beginner-level dataset from Kaggle and work on simple machine learning models.
- Start experimenting with basic algorithms like linear regression and decision trees.

Month 5-6: Focus on advanced topics.

- Take a deep dive into deep learning or natural language processing (NLP).
- Complete a more complex project—perhaps a sentiment analysis model or a facial recognition system.

By following this structured path and staying committed to learning and experimenting, you'll be on the fast track to becoming an AI professional. So, take a deep breath, set your intentions, and get started. The journey may seem daunting, but remember: the most successful AI professionals all started with the same mindset—**one step at a time**.

In the end, remember this: AI is a journey, not a destination. Stay curious, stay committed, and continue learning. The road ahead is filled with exciting opportunities, and your adventure into the world of AI is just beginning.

Chapter 5: Gaining Experience – Projects That Stand Out

When I first started working in AI, it wasn't just the certifications and courses that helped me get ahead—it was the real-world experience. I vividly remember the time when I was working on my first AI project. I had learned the theory, done the online courses, and understood the algorithms, but I was missing something crucial: the hands-on experience that would set me apart. The truth is, **theoretical knowledge is just one part of the equation**. To truly succeed in AI, you need to **gain real-world experience**—whether through internships, open-source contributions, or personal projects.

In this chapter, we'll dive into how to gain meaningful experience, which projects you can work on to stand out, and how to present those projects effectively to potential employers. Let's walk through this journey together, step by step, and I'll show you how the experience you gain today can make a lasting impact on your career tomorrow.

1. The Importance of Internships and Open-Source Contributions

When I think back on my early career, one of the most transformative experiences I had was during my **first internship**. I was still in the learning phase, just like many of you, and I felt overwhelmed by how much I still didn't know. But the moment I entered a real-world AI project, everything started to click.

Internships: The Gateway to Practical Experience

Internships provide you with the opportunity to work in an actual AI-driven environment, where you'll see how the theoretical concepts are applied in real-world settings. As someone who's been part of AI projects for years, I can tell you this: **internships aren't just about gaining experience for your resume**; they are about **immersing yourself in the challenges, the problem-solving, and the innovation that AI brings to the table.**

Let's take a moment to talk about **Ravi**, a fresh graduate who had recently completed his AI certification. Ravi had always dreamed of working at a top tech company, but he didn't know how to get his foot in the door. After several months of applying to positions, he decided to take a different approach: **internships**.

He applied for a **Data Science internship** at a mid-sized healthcare tech company. Even though he wasn't fully confident in his skills, he felt it was the right step. Within the first few weeks, Ravi was put on a project where he had to work with patient data and predict the likelihood of readmissions. His knowledge of machine learning came into play as he worked with the company's senior data scientists, who mentored him through every step of the process.

What Ravi learned was invaluable—not just about the tools, but also about how the business uses data to make decisions. That internship became his gateway into a full-time position at the company. **The hands-on experience he gained in that environment was far more valuable than anything he could have learned in a classroom.**

If you're looking to gain experience, internships are an absolute must. They provide **real-world exposure**, allow you to **build your professional network**, and show future employers that you're capable of handling real challenges. Whether it's with a large company or a startup, an internship will add significant value to your resume.

Open-Source Contributions: Giving Back to the AI Community

One often-overlooked way to gain experience in AI is through **open-source contributions**. The beauty of open-source projects is that anyone, regardless of their experience level, can contribute to them. Whether you're fixing a bug, adding a feature, or optimizing an algorithm, your contributions will be a tangible way to demonstrate your skills to the world.

Take the example of **Priya**, a budding AI enthusiast. Priya had just completed a few beginner-level courses on machine learning, but she was struggling to find her place in the industry. One day, she stumbled upon an open-source **NLP (Natural Language Processing)** project on GitHub. The project was aimed at building a chatbot that could automatically respond to customer queries for a retail company.

Priya decided to dive in. At first, she contributed small bug fixes and improved the code documentation. As she gained confidence, she tackled more complex issues, such as improving the bot's response accuracy by incorporating **BERT** (Bidirectional Encoder Representations from Transformers), a popular deep learning model for NLP. Over the next few months, Priya not only honed her skills but also built her reputation within the open-source community. Her contributions were recognized by the project maintainers, and she was invited to collaborate with them on more significant features.

Priya's work on GitHub became an integral part of her portfolio when she started applying for jobs. **Open-source contributions allowed her to gain practical experience, collaborate with experts, and build a network of professionals—all of which played a crucial role in landing her first full-time job as an AI Engineer.**

2. Real-World Scenarios: Projects That Add Value

I can tell you from personal experience that the projects you work on can make or break your chances in AI. When it comes to building your portfolio, it's essential to choose **projects that solve real problems** and demonstrate your ability to apply AI concepts to **tangible use cases**.

Let's break down a few **real-world scenarios** that can help you get started.

Sentiment Analysis: Understanding Customer Feedback

Sentiment analysis is one of the most popular AI projects, especially for beginners. It involves analyzing text (usually social media posts, reviews, or comments) to determine whether the sentiment is positive, negative, or neutral. Many companies use sentiment analysis to gauge customer feedback and improve their products or services.

For instance, imagine you're working with a startup that sells eco-friendly products. You've gathered thousands of customer reviews from different online platforms, and your task is to build a model that analyzes the sentiment behind each review. If the review contains words like "love," "great," or "fantastic," it's categorized as positive; if it contains words like "disappointed" or "poor," it's classified as negative.

Not only does this project demonstrate your understanding of **NLP** and **text classification**, but it also shows that you can **use AI to solve real business problems**. It's a project you can proudly showcase on your resume, and it can serve as a great conversation starter in interviews.

Chatbots: Revolutionizing Customer Support

Chatbots are another great project to add to your portfolio. Companies use chatbots for **customer support,** allowing them to answer frequently asked questions, book appointments, and even process orders. By building a chatbot, you're demonstrating that you understand how AI can streamline business operations and improve customer experience.

Let's say you're working on a chatbot for an online food delivery service. The chatbot is programmed to understand customer queries like "Where is my order?" or "Can I modify my delivery address?" The more sophisticated the chatbot, the better you'll showcase your understanding of AI-driven conversational systems. You might even integrate it with **natural language processing (NLP)** techniques like **intent classification** and **entity recognition**.

Through this project, you'll gain a deeper understanding of how machine learning models can be applied to **real-time problems** and how AI-driven automation can save companies both time and money. Plus, chatbots are an excellent addition to your portfolio as they are highly visible to potential employers.

3. How to Present Your Projects Effectively

Now that you've worked on some great projects, the next step is to showcase them in a way that grabs the attention of potential employers. **How you present your work can make all the difference.**

Documenting Your Projects

A key part of presenting your projects is **documentation**. Employers want to understand your thought process and see how you approach problems. You don't just want to share your final solution—you want to explain the steps you took to get there.

- **Write detailed READMEs**: Include a high-level description of the project, its goals, and how you solved the problem.
- **Share your code on GitHub**: Ensure your code is well-organized and easy to navigate. Make sure you include comments that explain complex sections.
- **Showcase results with visualizations**: Use graphs and charts to visualize the results of your project. If you built a chatbot, show a demo of the chatbot in action or include screenshots that highlight its functionality.

Creating a Personal Website or Portfolio

Having a **personal website** is another great way to showcase your AI projects. A website allows you to have all your work in one place, and it provides you with an opportunity to present your portfolio in a **clean, professional manner**. Include your **GitHub link, project descriptions**, and **case studies** that demonstrate how your projects add value.

Sophie, an AI graduate who I mentored, took this step early in her career. She built a simple website that showcased her projects, including a sentiment analysis tool she had built for a retail company. Sophie added a section detailing her contributions to several open-source projects, and this site became her **digital resume**. In interviews, she would simply share the link, and potential employers were immediately impressed by her ability to present her work professionally.

4. Interactive Exercise – Presenting Your First AI Project

By now, you should have at least one project in your portfolio. It could be a sentiment analysis, a chatbot, or something else entirely. The next step is to present it effectively.

Here's an exercise for you: **Take one of your AI projects and document it as if you're applying for your dream job**. Write a detailed README, add visualizations, and organize the project files. Create a section on your personal website or portfolio to showcase it, and practice presenting your work to a mock interview panel (maybe your friends or peers).

Conclusion

As you continue your journey in AI, remember this: **Experience is everything**. Internships, open-source contributions, and personal projects will give you the practical skills and real-world knowledge that can't be learned from textbooks alone. The projects you work on today will set the foundation for your career tomorrow. And as Henry David Thoreau said, "Success usually comes to those who are too busy to be looking for it." Focus on building valuable projects, and success will follow.

Stay curious, keep learning, and always strive to make your work **impactful**. Your journey in AI is just beginning, and the opportunities are limitless. Keep pushing the boundaries, one project at a time.

Chapter 6: The AI Professional's Toolkit

When I first ventured into AI, the tools and platforms I used were almost like my toolbox—the right tools would help me build solutions, break down complex problems, and bring my ideas to life. Today, as an AI professional, I can confidently say that **having the right toolkit** is one of the most important factors in your success. Whether you're an aspiring AI professional, transitioning into AI from another field, or someone already working in the domain, understanding and mastering the tools available is key to creating real-world, scalable solutions.

In this chapter, we'll walk through the essential tools and platforms that every AI professional needs in their toolkit, with real-life examples of how they are used. You'll also learn how to set up your development environment effectively, so you can dive into building your own AI models with confidence.

1. Must-Know Tools and Platforms: TensorFlow, PyTorch, Jupyter Notebooks, and More

There's a vast ecosystem of tools available to AI professionals today. However, there are a few core platforms and libraries that have become industry standards. Let's explore some of the most important tools that will help you craft AI solutions with ease.

TensorFlow: Powering Deep Learning Models

When I first started working with AI, **TensorFlow** was a game-changer for me. It's an open-source library developed by Google and is widely used for building machine learning and deep learning models. TensorFlow is highly flexible and scalable, which means it can be used for everything from basic machine learning models to complex neural networks for tasks like image recognition or natural language processing.

Let me take you back to **Amit**, a software engineer who had been working in traditional software development for years. Amit had always been interested in AI but was intimidated by the complexity of deep learning. After taking a deep dive into the TensorFlow tutorials and documentation, he slowly started applying his knowledge to real projects.

One of the first projects he worked on was a **digit recognition system** using the **MNIST dataset** (a classic dataset of handwritten digits). Amit used TensorFlow to train a neural network and achieved impressive results. What he didn't expect was the **career transformation** that followed. His deep learning project caught the attention of a top AI-driven startup, and he was offered a position as an AI engineer.

TensorFlow was the tool that helped him bridge the gap between his software engineering background and the world of AI. It opened doors to career opportunities he had never imagined. **Mastering TensorFlow** can be your gateway to similar transformations. The library is powerful, scalable, and continuously evolving, so it's worth investing your time and effort in mastering it.

PyTorch: The Researcher's Choice

While TensorFlow has been a go-to platform for production-ready models, **PyTorch** has gained tremendous popularity among researchers and AI practitioners who are working on cutting-edge solutions. PyTorch is favored for its ease of use, dynamic computational graph, and fast prototyping capabilities.

I vividly recall my experience with PyTorch during a deep learning project aimed at building a recommendation system for a client in the retail industry. While TensorFlow is fantastic for building large, production-ready systems, PyTorch's ability to quickly modify and experiment with model architectures allowed me to make rapid iterations.

A **real-life example** of someone leveraging PyTorch is **Sanya**, a data scientist who transitioned from a non-technical background in economics. Sanya was always fascinated by AI, but she struggled to understand the technical aspects of machine learning. She decided to focus on learning PyTorch, and over the course of several months, she built a model to predict customer churn for a telecommunications company. PyTorch's flexible architecture made it easier for her to test different neural network configurations.

Her success story didn't end there. **Sanya's ability to understand and apply deep learning algorithms with PyTorch** led to a job offer at a leading AI consultancy firm, where she now works on state-of-the-art research projects. PyTorch was the tool that helped her go from a curious beginner to a capable AI practitioner.

Jupyter Notebooks: The Ultimate Tool for Exploration

As an AI professional, **Jupyter Notebooks** will become your best friend. It's an open-source web application that allows you to create and share live code, equations, visualizations, and narrative text. It's one of the best tools for experimenting with code and prototyping machine learning models.

Let's take **Arjun**, for example. He was a student who recently completed his degree in computer science but wasn't quite sure how to jump into AI. During his summer break, he started experimenting with Jupyter Notebooks to build simple models on datasets from Kaggle. Jupyter provided him with an interactive platform where he could test hypotheses, visualize data, and make quick changes to his models—all within the same environment.

Arjun went on to build a **credit scoring model** for a fintech startup using Jupyter Notebooks. His ability to present the code alongside charts and data visualizations made it much easier for the company to understand the model's inner workings. The interactive nature of Jupyter Notebooks allowed Arjun to present his findings in a way that was accessible even to non-technical stakeholders.

Jupyter Notebooks is a fantastic tool for **data exploration, model prototyping**, and **presentation**. It allows you to blend code and insights seamlessly, making it an invaluable part of any AI professional's toolkit.

Scikit-learn: The Swiss Army Knife of Machine Learning

If you're just starting out with machine learning, you'll quickly come across **Scikit-learn**—a Python library that provides simple and efficient tools for data mining and data analysis. It is built on top of **NumPy, SciPy**, and **matplotlib**, which means it integrates well with other scientific libraries.

One of the key features of Scikit-learn is its wide range of pre-built algorithms for classification, regression, clustering, and dimensionality reduction. For **newcomers**, Scikit-learn offers an excellent starting point for implementing machine learning models without the complexity of deep learning frameworks.

Take the story of **Samir**, a recent computer science graduate who didn't have the luxury of diving into deep learning immediately. Instead, he started building machine learning models using Scikit-learn. One of his first projects was to predict house prices based on various features like square footage, number of bedrooms, and location. Using Scikit-learn, he was able to quickly train models like **linear regression** and **decision trees**, and with each project, his confidence grew.

For Samir, Scikit-learn was his gateway into AI, and it helped him land his first job as a machine learning engineer. **It's a great tool for quickly prototyping models** and building a solid foundation in machine learning principles before moving on to more complex techniques.

2. Hands-On Tips: Setting Up Your AI Development Environment

By now, you've likely seen how these tools play a role in solving real-world problems, but how do you set yourself up for success? How do you create the **right environment** to start experimenting with AI?

Let's walk through the process of setting up a development environment for AI, step by step.

Step 1: Install Python and Jupyter Notebooks

The first thing you'll need is Python—**the primary language for AI** development. To get started, follow these steps:

1. **Install Anaconda**: Anaconda is a popular Python distribution that comes with Jupyter Notebooks, SciPy, NumPy, pandas, and many other data science libraries pre-installed.
    - Download Anaconda from the official site and follow the installation instructions for your operating system (Windows, macOS, Linux).
    - After installation, launch **Anaconda Navigator**, which provides a user-friendly interface to manage environments and packages.
2. **Install Jupyter Notebooks**:
    - If you installed Anaconda, Jupyter is already included. To launch Jupyter, open the **Anaconda Navigator** and click "Launch" under Jupyter Notebooks.

Step 2: Set Up TensorFlow or PyTorch

To start working with deep learning models, you'll need to install a framework like **TensorFlow** or **PyTorch**. Here's how:

1. **Install TensorFlow**:
   - Open your terminal (or Anaconda Prompt) and type the following command:
   - pip install tensorflow
2. **Install PyTorch**:
   - If you choose to work with PyTorch, you can install it using:
   - pip install torch torchvision

Step 3: Install Other Useful Libraries

For data manipulation and visualization, there are several libraries you should install:

1. **pandas** – For handling datasets.
   1. pip install pandas
2. **matplotlib** – For plotting graphs and visualizations.
   1. pip install matplotlib
3. **scikit-learn** – For building machine learning models.
   1. pip install scikit-learn

Step 4: Test Your Environment

Once you have all the tools installed, create a simple script to test if everything is working correctly:

import tensorflow as tf

print("TensorFlow version:", tf.__version__)

```
import torch
print("PyTorch version:", torch.__version__)
import pandas as pd
print("pandas version:", pd.__version__)
```

If this script runs successfully, you're all set up to start building AI models.

Conclusion: Building Your AI Future

Equipped with these tools and resources, you're now ready to tackle the world of AI. The tools we've discussed—**TensorFlow, PyTorch, Jupyter Notebooks, Scikit-learn**—are just the tip of the iceberg, but mastering them will provide a solid foundation for your career in AI.

As AI continues to evolve, so will the tools and platforms available to you. However, the most important thing to remember is this: **The tools are just that—tools.** What truly matters is how you use them to solve real problems. The more you practice, the more intuitive these tools will become.

So, go ahead—dive into these tools, experiment, and begin building your own AI projects. Just like **Amit**, **Sanya**, and **Arjun**, you too can turn your learning into career success. The future is in your hands, and with the right toolkit, there's no limit to what you can achieve.

Chapter 7: Building a Personal Brand in AI

In the fast-paced and constantly evolving world of artificial intelligence (AI), knowledge alone isn't enough to stand out. **Building a personal brand**—one that reflects your expertise, passion, and contributions—is equally important. AI is no longer just a niche skill set; it has become a field with vast opportunities, and **those who are able to showcase their unique strengths** and insights are the ones who rise to the top.

I remember when I first started in AI. It wasn't just about learning algorithms or writing code; I quickly realized that it was about **sharing my journey**, **showing my progress**, and most importantly, **connecting with others** who were on similar paths. The more I shared, the more I learned. The more I learned, the more opportunities came my way. That's how I began to build my own personal brand in AI.

In this chapter, we will explore how you can establish and grow your personal brand in AI. Through powerful platforms like LinkedIn, GitHub, and Kaggle, you can not only showcase your expertise but also open doors to countless career opportunities. Additionally, we'll look at networking strategies that will help you build relationships with industry leaders and peers. Finally, we'll explore the journey of a professional who transformed from being relatively unknown to becoming a respected AI thought leader.

1. The Role of LinkedIn, GitHub, and Kaggle in Showcasing Expertise

As you embark on your AI journey, it's critical to build an online presence that showcases your skills and accomplishments. Let's take a closer look at the **top platforms** that can help you do that: **LinkedIn**, **GitHub**, and **Kaggle**.

LinkedIn: The Professional Network

LinkedIn is a powerful platform for professionals to showcase their careers, share content, and connect with peers in their industry. But simply having a profile isn't enough—it's how you use it that matters.

I vividly remember meeting **Suresh**, a young data scientist, at an AI conference a few years ago. When I looked him up on LinkedIn, I was impressed by how he presented himself. Suresh regularly posted about his AI projects, shared insights from the latest research papers he was reading, and even wrote articles about trends in deep learning and natural language processing. His LinkedIn profile was filled with rich content that demonstrated his expertise, but it was his **consistent engagement with the community** that truly set him apart.

One of the most impactful ways to build your personal brand on LinkedIn is to share your journey. Whether you're working on a **machine learning project**, learning a new framework, or attending an AI conference, let your network know about it. Share lessons learned, challenges faced, and breakthroughs achieved. **Content**—whether it's a thoughtful post, a project update, or an article—can help you build credibility and **position yourself as an active participant in the AI community**.

GitHub: The Developer's Portfolio

GitHub is more than just a place to store your code; it's a **showcase of your development skills** and a testament to your work ethic. When I look at a GitHub profile, I immediately get a sense of the individual's coding style, commitment to open-source contributions, and ability to collaborate. **Projects on GitHub** speak louder than any resume ever could. It's a place where your code becomes a living, breathing reflection of your expertise.

Take **Priya**, a former teacher who made a bold career switch into AI. When Priya started learning machine learning, she wasn't sure where to showcase her skills. She heard about GitHub from a fellow learner and decided to upload her small projects, like **predictive models using simple datasets**. Over time, she began contributing to open-source machine learning projects and collaborated with other developers on GitHub. Today, Priya is a senior AI engineer at a leading tech firm, and her GitHub profile is a major part of her professional identity. Employers often reference her GitHub to see how well she codes, collaborates, and contributes to the AI community.

By contributing to projects, building your own repositories, and participating in **open-source communities**, GitHub can help you **demonstrate your capabilities** to the world. It's an online **portfolio** that proves your hands-on experience and problem-solving skills.

Kaggle: Showcasing Problem-Solving Skills Through Competitions

Kaggle is often referred to as the "**Olympics of Data Science**" due to its highly competitive nature. It's a platform where data scientists and machine learning practitioners come together to solve real-world problems. I've met several professionals who've used Kaggle not just to improve their skills but also to get noticed by employers.

Take **Ravi**, a software engineer who was interested in making the leap into AI. While his job involved programming, he didn't have much hands-on experience in machine learning. To improve his skills and get noticed, Ravi started competing in Kaggle competitions. Over time, he gained experience by solving real-world problems and improving his rankings. One of his Kaggle notebooks on sentiment analysis caught the attention of a recruiter from a major tech company, and soon after, Ravi was offered a role as a machine learning engineer. Today, his **Kaggle profile** is an impressive testament to his problem-solving abilities and his ability to tackle complex challenges.

Kaggle is also a great place to learn from others. **Look at the kernels (code notebooks)** shared by other professionals, participate in discussions, and learn from the solutions provided by top performers. As you build your own reputation through consistent contributions and high-ranking competition entries, **Kaggle can become a key part of your personal brand.**

2. Networking Tips: Participating in AI Conferences and Hackathons

A strong personal brand isn't just about showcasing your work online; it's also about **building relationships** with others in the AI community. Networking is one of the most effective ways to grow your career and gain new opportunities.

AI Conferences: Building Connections and Learning from Experts

AI conferences are one of the best places to network with industry professionals, share your knowledge, and learn from experts. Whether it's a massive event like **NeurIPS** or a smaller, niche conference, these events provide great opportunities to meet like-minded individuals and gain insights into the latest trends in AI.

I remember attending a **Deep Learning conference** a few years ago, where I met **Vikram**, a data scientist from a well-known e-commerce company. Vikram wasn't a well-known name in the industry at the time, but he had an impressive **understanding of reinforcement learning**. We hit it off immediately, and over the next few months, we continued to exchange ideas and collaborate on various projects. What stood out about Vikram was his willingness to engage with other professionals, share his experiences, and seek feedback. **This proactive approach** helped him build a strong network within the AI community, which eventually led to new opportunities and career advancements.

By attending conferences, speaking at events, or simply joining conversations, you put yourself in a position to be **discovered by key players** in AI. Don't be afraid to introduce yourself, ask questions, or even share your own experiences—people are always looking to connect with passionate individuals.

Hackathons: Showcasing Your Skills in Real-World Challenges

Hackathons are another excellent way to build your personal brand. They provide the perfect environment for you to test your skills, collaborate with others, and showcase your ability to build practical, real-world AI solutions. Many AI professionals have built strong reputations by excelling in hackathons, where their solutions have caught the attention of potential employers and collaborators.

I had the pleasure of working alongside **Aisha** at a **24-hour AI hackathon** hosted by a major tech company. Aisha, a recent graduate in computer science, had just started learning AI. She was initially unsure of her skills, but during the hackathon, her passion for solving real-world problems shone through. She used natural language processing to build an AI-powered chatbot in just one day. Not only did Aisha's team win the competition, but the company also offered her a full-time position, recognizing her technical ability and problem-solving mindset. **Hackathons gave Aisha the platform** to demonstrate her skills and make valuable connections, ultimately launching her career in AI.

Participating in hackathons can also be an excellent way to **build your portfolio**. Even if you don't win, the experience you gain and the projects you complete are valuable assets that contribute to your personal brand.

3. Case Study: From Obscurity to Thought Leader

Let me tell you the story of **Manish**, a man who started from humble beginnings in AI and eventually became a well-respected thought leader. When Manish first entered the field, he was working in a small tech startup in a city where AI wasn't exactly the most talked-about field. He had a passion for machine learning but wasn't sure how to get noticed.

Manish began by **building a strong presence on LinkedIn**, where he shared detailed posts about his personal projects and insights from AI research papers. At first, not many people noticed him. But instead of giving up, he decided to **stay consistent**. He joined Kaggle competitions and shared his results, even though he was still learning. Slowly but surely, Manish started to gain recognition.

As his knowledge deepened, he started speaking at **local tech meetups** and contributing to open-source projects on GitHub. Over time, he gained a reputation for his ability to break down complex AI concepts into easily digestible content. He even started his own blog, where he wrote articles about AI trends and innovations. His **willingness to share**—whether it was through LinkedIn, Kaggle, or his blog—allowed him to connect with professionals all over the world.

Today, Manish is a **recognized AI thought leader** with thousands of followers on LinkedIn and a growing network of collaborators. He is often invited to speak at AI conferences and has even started his own consulting company. **Manish's story** is a perfect example of how building a personal brand in AI requires **consistency, passion**, and a willingness to **share your knowledge** with others.

Conclusion

Building a personal brand in AI is not an overnight process. It takes time, effort, and a commitment to sharing your journey, learning from others, and networking with like-minded individuals. Whether it's through **LinkedIn**, **GitHub**, **Kaggle**, or **conferences**, you have numerous platforms at your disposal to **showcase your expertise** and build valuable relationships.

Remember, as Jeff Bezos wisely said, *"Your brand is what other people say about you when you're not in the room."* Your brand is not just about what you know, but about how you share that knowledge, how you engage with others, and how you build a reputation as a **go-to expert** in the AI field.

So, don't wait for opportunities to come to you. **Create your own opportunities** by building your personal brand, sharing your work, and connecting with the AI community. The future of AI is bright, and by building your personal brand today, you'll be prepared to take full advantage of the exciting opportunities ahead.

Chapter 8: Overcoming Challenges and Staying Motivated

Starting a career in AI is an exciting journey, but it's not without its fair share of challenges. As much as we talk about the opportunities and the potential of AI, we often overlook the **personal struggles** that come with trying to break into such a competitive and rapidly evolving field. In this chapter, we'll explore some of the most common obstacles aspiring AI professionals face, how to overcome them, and how to stay motivated even when things get tough.

When I first decided to pursue AI, I knew it would be challenging. The learning curve was steep, and the technology was constantly evolving. At times, it felt like I was drowning in a sea of information—new programming languages, new algorithms, new tools, and new breakthroughs happening every day. But as I reflect on my own journey, I realize that what truly helped me **push through the hard times** was my mindset, my ability to stay motivated, and most importantly, the understanding that I wasn't alone in facing these challenges.

In this chapter, we'll dive deep into **three major challenges** that many people face when they're working to build a career in AI—**imposter syndrome**, **learning fatigue**, and **the struggle to stay updated**. We'll also look at a real-life example of someone who faced these challenges head-on and emerged stronger, and finally, I'll offer an interactive exercise to help you stay motivated on your AI journey.

Common Challenges

Imposter Syndrome: The Silent Struggle

One of the most pervasive challenges many AI professionals face, especially when they are starting out, is **imposter syndrome**. This is the feeling that you're not good enough, that you don't belong, or that you're somehow "faking it." It's that voice inside your head that tells you that your achievements are a fluke or that everyone else around you knows more than you. It's a feeling that you're just **pretending** to be someone you're not.

I remember the first time I attended a large AI conference. The room was filled with **world-renowned experts**, and as I sat there listening to their discussions, I couldn't help but feel like I didn't belong. I thought to myself, "How could I, a relative newcomer to AI, ever contribute to this field?" I struggled with the idea of whether I was truly capable of making a difference. This is imposter syndrome at its finest—believing you're not enough, despite all evidence to the contrary.

The good news is that imposter syndrome is incredibly common, especially in fields like AI, where new professionals are constantly surrounded by brilliant minds. But the key is recognizing that **everyone experiences imposter syndrome at some point**, even the people you admire. It's a natural part of growing and learning. Rather than letting it hold you back, you can use imposter syndrome as a **signal** that you are pushing yourself outside your comfort zone and growing as a professional.

Learning Fatigue: The Dreaded Overload

Another challenge that comes with building a career in AI is the feeling of **learning fatigue**. As you dive deeper into machine learning, data science, and AI, you might start to feel overwhelmed by the sheer amount of information that needs to be absorbed. You might find yourself learning a new concept one day, only to find that the next day, the **landscape has changed** again with a new breakthrough or a new framework that's now the "latest thing."

For instance, I remember spending weeks learning about **neural networks**—reading papers, taking courses, and practicing coding exercises. Just when I thought I was starting to get a handle on it, I found out about a newer, more efficient type of neural network called **transformers**, which were rapidly gaining popularity. I felt like I had just caught up, only to realize I had to start over. It was frustrating.

Learning fatigue can take a toll on your motivation. The constant pressure to keep up with new developments, the **endless resources** to sift through, and the **self-doubt** that creeps in when you feel like you're falling behind—these things can make you want to give up.

But here's the thing: **Learning in AI is a marathon, not a sprint.** The key to combating learning fatigue is setting realistic goals and creating a sustainable learning routine. You don't need to learn everything at once. Focus on small, manageable tasks, and allow yourself time to absorb and apply the knowledge. Progress, no matter how small, is still progress. And remember, **you don't have to know everything**. AI is a vast field, and specialization is important. Choose a niche that interests you and become deeply skilled in it.

Staying Updated: The Race Against Time

In the fast-paced world of AI, **staying updated** with the latest trends and developments is a constant challenge. New papers are published daily, new frameworks are released regularly, and the AI community is in a continuous state of flux. It can feel like you're always playing catch-up.

I remember one particular instance when I was trying to stay current with **AI research**. I would spend hours reading papers, watching webinars, and attending talks to stay on top of new advancements. But even after all that, I felt like I was falling behind because new research was being released faster than I could consume it. There was a moment when I realized that this wasn't sustainable. **I couldn't keep up with everything.** I had to make a decision to **focus** on the areas that were most relevant to my goals and interests.

Staying updated doesn't mean you need to know everything. It means being **strategic** in how you approach your learning. Follow key thought leaders on platforms like Twitter, LinkedIn, and Medium. Join relevant AI communities where you can discuss new ideas. Use tools like **Google Scholar** and **arXiv** to keep track of the latest papers in your area of interest. Staying updated is about **choosing your sources wisely** and absorbing information that adds value to your specific career path.

Real-Life Example: A Working Professional's Story of Resilience

To truly understand how to overcome these challenges, let me share the story of **Ankit**, a working professional who faced a number of obstacles when making the transition from a traditional software engineering role to an AI career. Ankit's story is one of **resilience**, and his journey shows how perseverance can lead to success.

Ankit was a software engineer at a large tech company, and although he was skilled in coding, he felt a strong desire to move into the AI field. He had always been fascinated by machine learning and data science, but he wasn't sure where to start. He began by taking online courses and reading books on AI. However, as he delved deeper, the challenges quickly became apparent.

Like many others, Ankit struggled with **imposter syndrome**. He found himself comparing his progress to that of experts in the field. When he went to AI meetups or read about AI breakthroughs, he felt like a small fish in a giant pond. The learning fatigue also hit him hard—he was learning about new algorithms and techniques, but he could never seem to keep up. And to make matters worse, the constant **pressure to stay updated** with new research added to his anxiety.

But Ankit didn't give up. He recognized that these challenges were a **normal part of the journey**. Instead of trying to master everything, he chose to focus on specific areas of AI that aligned with his interests, like **natural language processing (NLP)**. He began taking small, incremental steps, setting realistic goals, and building projects on platforms like Kaggle. He also started contributing to open-source projects, which helped him gain confidence and build his portfolio.

After several months of consistent effort, Ankit landed an internship at a leading AI firm. His success wasn't an overnight achievement. It was the result of his **resilience**—his ability to keep going, even when the road seemed steep and challenging. Today, Ankit is a full-time AI engineer, and his journey continues to inspire others who are facing similar challenges.

Interactive Exercise: Writing Your Personal AI Motivation Statement

Staying motivated is often about **finding your 'why'**—the reason that drives you to keep going, even when things get tough. An effective way to reconnect with your motivation is by writing a **Personal AI Motivation Statement**. This is a statement that captures the reasons you're passionate about AI, what you want to achieve, and how you plan to overcome challenges.

Here's how you can write your own motivation statement:

1. **Reflect on Your 'Why':** Why do you want to pursue a career in AI? Is it because you want to solve complex problems? Do you want to contribute to society through AI-powered innovations? Are you inspired by the potential of AI to change industries and improve lives? Write down your core reasons for pursuing this field.
2. **Acknowledge the Challenges:** Recognize that AI is a

challenging field. Acknowledge the obstacles you may face along the way—be it imposter syndrome, learning fatigue, or the difficulty of staying updated. Be honest about these challenges.
3. **Commit to Overcoming Obstacles:** Write down how you plan to **overcome these challenges**. Perhaps you'll focus on one project at a time to avoid learning fatigue, or you'll set aside regular time each week to stay updated with the latest trends in AI.
4. **Set Clear Goals:** What do you want to achieve in the next 6 months? 1 year? 5 years? Write down specific, measurable goals that will keep you on track.
5. **Create a Vision for Success:** Finally, paint a picture of what success looks like for you. Whether it's landing your first AI job, becoming a thought leader, or building a successful AI startup—write down your vision of success.

Conclusion

Overcoming challenges in AI is not just about mastering technical skills or acquiring new knowledge. It's about building **resilience**, staying **motivated**, and believing in your ability to succeed. **Imposter syndrome**, **learning fatigue**, and the constant battle to **stay updated** are all part of the journey. But as you keep pushing forward, you'll find that these challenges become stepping stones toward your success.

Remember, the road to a career in AI is a marathon, not a sprint. Take it one step at a time, stay true to your **motivation**, and always keep your eye on the bigger picture. By doing so, you'll not only overcome the challenges but also thrive in the exciting world of AI.

Chapter 9: Landing Your First Job or Transitioning into AI

Securing your first job in AI—or transitioning into an AI career from a different field—can be one of the most rewarding yet daunting milestones of your professional journey. As you begin to apply what you've learned, develop your skills, and gain confidence, the next step is to **enter the job market**. Whether you're a recent graduate or a professional seeking to pivot into AI, **getting that first offer** can feel like an elusive goal, especially given the competitive nature of the industry.

But here's the truth: **opportunities don't just happen—they're created.** The key to landing that first job in AI lies in how well you craft your profile, tailor your approach, and present yourself to potential employers. In this chapter, we'll cover everything from **resume tips** and **interview preparation** to real-life hiring stories and expert insights on how to stand out in a crowded field.

When I first transitioned into AI, I vividly remember the mixture of excitement and nerves I felt about my first job application. I had just completed my online courses, built a few basic projects, and felt like I was on the cusp of something great. But at the same time, I was worried. Was I ready? Would my experience in a different field count? Would I be able to stand out among the many highly qualified candidates? **The first job is often the hardest one to land**, but the process itself is a vital learning experience.

Let's break it down and give you a roadmap to **successfully land your first AI role** or **transition into an AI career** from a non-technical field.

1. Building a Resume That Stands Out

The first thing you need to understand is that your resume for an AI role is not just about listing **skills** and **experiences**. It's about telling your story in a way that highlights **your unique journey** and **value proposition** in the AI space.

Showcase Relevant Skills

While employers will want to see your technical skills (such as **machine learning**, **Python**, **TensorFlow**, **PyTorch**, etc.), they will also value **problem-solving** abilities, critical thinking, and communication skills. I recommend focusing on the following:

- **Programming**: List the languages you are proficient in—especially Python, R, or any other programming languages relevant to AI and machine learning.
- **Machine Learning**: Highlight any machine learning algorithms you are familiar with (e.g., supervised learning, deep learning, natural language processing).
- **Tools and Frameworks**: Be sure to list tools like **TensorFlow**, **PyTorch**, **scikit-learn**, and **Keras**. These are industry-standard tools that AI professionals frequently use.
- **Data Analysis**: Demonstrating familiarity with **data manipulation** tools (such as **Pandas** or **SQL**) and experience working with data will set you apart.
- **Project Experience**: Instead of simply listing theoretical knowledge, **show projects** you've worked on—whether personal projects, **Kaggle competitions**, or internships. These can make a huge difference in showcasing that you can apply your knowledge to real-world problems.

Structure Your Resume Effectively

Here's a **quick structure** for a strong AI resume:

- **Contact Information**: Full name, email, LinkedIn profile, GitHub, personal website (if applicable).
- **Objective Statement**: A clear, concise statement that defines your goals (e.g., "Aspiring AI engineer with a passion for solving real-world problems using machine learning and deep learning techniques. Seeking to apply my skills in a dynamic AI-driven company.").
- **Key Skills**: List your core technical skills (as mentioned above).
- **Projects**: Include a few of your most impressive projects, emphasizing the technologies used and the outcomes.
- **Education**: Mention any relevant degrees or certifications.
- **Work Experience**: If applicable, describe your work history, emphasizing transferable skills.
- **Certifications**: Include relevant certifications from platforms like **Coursera**, **Udemy**, or **edX**.
- **Achievements or Volunteer Work**: Mention any additional activities that demonstrate your dedication to AI (e.g., participation in AI meetups, contributions to open-source projects).

Make sure your resume is **tailored** to each job you apply for. Look closely at the job descriptions and ensure you reflect the keywords and skills they're looking for. Companies often use **applicant tracking systems (ATS)** that scan resumes for specific keywords, so this step is crucial.

2. Nailing the Interview

Once your resume gets you in the door, the **interview** becomes your chance to show your passion, problem-solving skills, and how well you fit within the organization. Here are some tips to help you succeed:

Understand the Role and the Company

Before the interview, research the company and the specific AI role you are applying for. Get familiar with their **products**, their **AI initiatives**, and the **technologies** they use. Tailor your responses to show how your skills align with the company's objectives. If possible, try to learn about the **team dynamics**, as working in AI often involves collaboration with diverse groups, such as data scientists, product managers, and engineers.

Technical Questions

You can expect **technical questions** that test your understanding of AI concepts. Here's how to prepare:

- **Review Core Concepts**: Revisit the fundamentals of machine learning algorithms, neural networks, and data science concepts. Brush up on **statistics**, **probability**, and **linear algebra**, as these are critical to AI.
- **Prepare for Coding Challenges**: Be ready to tackle coding challenges on platforms like **LeetCode**, **HackerRank**, or **Codewars**. Companies often ask for coding exercises to gauge your problem-solving and coding proficiency. Practice **algorithmic thinking** and **coding in Python** regularly.
- **Explain Your Projects**: Be prepared to walk the interviewer through the **projects** you've worked on. Talk about the **problem**, the **approach** you took, the **tools** you used, and the **outcome**. Use this as an opportunity to demonstrate your practical skills and ability to apply theory to real-world problems.

Behavioral Questions

Along with technical questions, expect **behavioral questions** that evaluate how you work with others and handle challenges. These might include questions like:

- "Tell me about a time you overcame a difficult problem."
- "How do you prioritize tasks when working on multiple projects?"
- "How do you approach learning new tools or techniques?"

When answering these questions, use the **STAR method** (Situation, Task, Action, Result) to structure your responses and clearly showcase your skills and achievements.

Ask Questions

Remember, interviews are a two-way street. Be sure to ask insightful questions about the role, team, and company culture. Questions like:

- "What does a typical day look like for someone in this role?"
- "How does the team approach problem-solving and collaboration?"
- "What AI-related challenges is the company currently facing?"

These questions show that you're not only interested in the job but also in how you can contribute and grow within the organization.

3. Real-Life Hiring Stories: From Struggles to Success

I want to share a few real-life stories of individuals who successfully landed their AI roles, despite facing significant hurdles. Their stories offer inspiration and tangible lessons you can apply to your own journey.

Story 1: From Data Analyst to Machine Learning Engineer

Take **Priya**, a data analyst working in a mid-sized company. She was passionate about AI but had very little experience with machine learning. After several years of analyzing data and building reports, Priya decided it was time to transition into the AI space.

She started by taking online courses, focusing on machine learning and deep learning. However, during her job search, Priya found that many companies wanted candidates with **direct AI experience**—something she didn't have. But Priya didn't let this discourage her. Instead, she focused on **transferable skills**—her experience working with data, her knowledge of programming, and her analytical thinking.

Priya revamped her resume, highlighting the projects she had completed during her courses, including a **prediction model** she developed using real-world data. She applied to multiple positions and finally landed an interview with a tech startup. During the interview, she impressed the hiring manager with her **ability to explain complex machine learning concepts** clearly and her **hands-on experience** with real-world data.

Priya's story shows that while transitioning to a new field may be challenging, **focus on your transferable skills**, demonstrate your eagerness to learn, and emphasize practical experience—even if it's gained outside of a formal job setting.

Story 2: From Sales to AI Researcher

Then there's **Sahil**, who had spent five years in sales before realizing that his true passion was AI. He had a basic understanding of coding but had no formal background in computer science. Sahil enrolled in a **bootcamp** to learn machine learning but faced skepticism when applying to AI roles due to his non-technical background.

However, Sahil didn't give up. He created a **portfolio of personal projects** and actively contributed to open-source AI projects. He also built an impressive GitHub repository showcasing his machine learning models and algorithms. After several months of networking and learning, Sahil landed his first AI internship, where he got to work on cutting-edge research.

Sahil's journey is a reminder that **perseverance and initiative** go a long way in AI, even if you're starting from a completely different field.

4. Quote: "Opportunities Don't Happen. You Create Them." – Chris Grosser

As you approach the final stages of your journey to landing your AI job, remember Chris Grosser's words: **"Opportunities don't happen. You create them."** Success in AI is not about waiting for the perfect job to come your way but about **taking proactive steps**, **building a strong network**, **showcasing your work**, and **constantly learning**.

The AI industry is full of **opportunity**—but you have to be ready to seize it. Keep working hard, keep experimenting, and never stop learning. Your dream job is out there, but it's up to you to create the path that will lead you to it.

Conclusion: Turning Aspirations into Reality

Landing your first AI job or making a career transition may seem daunting, but with the right strategies in place, you can overcome any obstacle. The **resume, interview**, and **networking** steps are all about telling your story effectively and demonstrating how you can add value to the company's AI initiatives.

Remember, the journey is long and sometimes challenging, but **every step you take** brings you closer to your goal. Whether it's gaining experience through internships, contributing to open-source projects, or mastering essential AI tools, each effort compounds into something greater.

By taking **ownership of your career, building a strong personal brand**, and **continuously upskilling**, you'll set yourself on the path to becoming a successful AI professional.

Chapter 10: Growing Your Career in AI

The world of Artificial Intelligence (AI) is a constantly evolving landscape, where **change is the only constant**. As you stand on the threshold of your AI career, excited by the possibilities that lie ahead, you may wonder: **How can I continue to grow in this field?** How do I stay relevant and move beyond just mastering the technical skills into taking on leadership roles? How do I transition from being a practitioner to someone who shapes the future of AI at the **strategic level**? These are all essential questions that you will begin to ask yourself as your career progresses. In this chapter, we will explore the journey of **lifelong learning**, the importance of **staying updated with emerging trends**, and the **path from practitioner to leader** in AI.

To grow in AI, you need to embrace the idea that your learning is never done. You will need to adapt to new technologies, **shift with the times**, and **upskill** constantly. The AI ecosystem is teeming with new opportunities, particularly as new fields like **Generative AI** continue to disrupt industries and transform the way businesses and individuals work. This chapter is about understanding how to ride that wave of change and **unlock the potential** for further growth in your AI career.

1. Lifelong Learning – Staying Updated with Emerging Trends

AI is a dynamic field, and to remain competitive, you must embrace a mindset of **lifelong learning**. The pace at which new research, tools, and breakthroughs are emerging in AI is staggering. Consider the incredible strides made in areas like **Generative AI**, **AI ethics**, and **reinforcement learning** over just the last few years. What was considered cutting-edge just a few months ago can be out of date by the time you complete a project.

Let's think about **Generative AI**, which has recently captured the imagination of the tech world. Whether it's through applications like **ChatGPT** or **image generation tools** like **DALL·E** or **MidJourney**, these technologies are reshaping industries such as entertainment, marketing, and even customer service. If you're an AI professional or aspiring to be one, understanding the **foundational principles of Generative AI** will position you as a thought leader in this space.

Staying Relevant in a Changing World

Take **Aditi**, a machine learning engineer who joined a startup in 2020. Initially, Aditi's work was centered around building traditional machine learning models using supervised learning. She quickly became proficient in **model building, data wrangling**, and **evaluation techniques**. However, as she observed the rapid rise of **Generative AI** in 2023, Aditi realized that she needed to **expand her skillset** if she wanted to continue being relevant.

Determined not to fall behind, she took it upon herself to learn the latest developments in generative models, particularly **GANs (Generative Adversarial Networks)**, **transformers**, and **large language models**. Aditi completed online certifications, participated in AI hackathons, and began contributing to open-source projects focused on **language models** and **AI creativity**. She also subscribed to **AI research journals** and followed thought leaders in the AI community, staying abreast of new trends, tools, and practices.

Her dedication paid off. Within a year, Aditi's knowledge of Generative AI became a crucial asset for her company, which was exploring ways to integrate creative AI models into its content generation process. She became a go-to expert in the field and was soon promoted to a **Lead AI Engineer**. The lesson here is clear: To grow in AI, you must be committed to continuous learning, especially as the field evolves at such a rapid pace.

How to Stay Updated

Here's how you can stay updated and continue growing:

- **Follow Thought Leaders and AI Communities**: Social media platforms like Twitter, LinkedIn, and GitHub are excellent resources for staying up to date. Thought leaders in AI often share the latest trends, papers, and discussions.
- **Subscribe to AI Journals and Blogs**: Keep yourself informed by reading papers, blog posts, and industry news. Websites like **arXiv**, **Medium**, and **Google AI Blog** are great starting points.
- **Engage in AI Conferences and Webinars**: Conferences like **NeurIPS**, **ICML**, and **CVPR** are where the AI community gathers to present the latest research and innovations. These events are invaluable for networking and learning.
- **Online Courses**: Platforms like **Coursera**, **edX**, and **Udacity** offer specialized courses that teach the most current AI technologies and concepts.
- **Hands-On Projects**: There's no better way to learn than by applying what you've learned to real-world problems. Contribute to open-source projects, participate in Kaggle competitions, or start personal projects.

2. From Practitioner to Strategist – Evolving into Leadership Roles

As you gain experience, you'll inevitably reach a point where your technical skills will no longer be the sole focus of your career. If you want to **move into leadership positions**, you'll need to develop a broader skill set that includes **strategic thinking**, **people management**, and a deep understanding of how AI can drive business outcomes. This shift from a technical practitioner to a strategic leader is one of the most exciting and rewarding transitions in any career.

The Leadership Journey

Take **Vikram**, a data scientist who worked in a consulting firm for nearly eight years. Vikram started his career as an AI practitioner, focused on delivering model development projects. He was great at writing complex algorithms and building data pipelines, but as his career progressed, he began to realize that his aspirations were growing beyond just delivering technical solutions.

Vikram was keen on **leading AI projects**, not just executing them. He wanted to help shape the strategic direction of his company's AI initiatives. So, he started taking on more responsibilities—mentoring junior data scientists, coordinating cross-functional teams, and participating in client meetings to discuss how AI could add value to their business goals.

Over time, Vikram's ability to connect AI solutions to business outcomes helped him transition into a **leadership role** as the **Head of AI Strategy**. In this role, he didn't just focus on algorithms anymore; he worked closely with the C-suite to align AI initiatives with the company's broader business objectives. This move from being a **data scientist** to a **strategic AI leader** involved a significant shift in mindset, but it was a path that many practitioners can take once they have honed their technical expertise.

Key Skills for Leadership in AI

To make this shift from a practitioner to a strategist, you need to develop the following skills:

- **Business Acumen**: Understand the business side of AI. This involves learning about ROI, business strategy, and how AI can **transform business models**. It's crucial to be able to speak the language of **stakeholders**.

- **Communication**: As a leader, you'll need to clearly communicate complex AI concepts to non-technical team members and executives. Being able to **simplify AI jargon** is a valuable skill.
- **Team Leadership and Mentorship**: Leading a team of AI professionals requires the ability to guide, motivate, and mentor your team. This includes managing diverse personalities, fostering collaboration, and setting clear expectations.
- **Strategic Thinking**: A good AI leader must think about **long-term goals** and how AI can be used as a competitive advantage. They must make decisions that align with the company's mission, vision, and objectives.
- **Cross-Disciplinary Collaboration**: AI leaders often work closely with other departments, such as marketing, product, and operations. Developing the ability to collaborate across departments is crucial for success.

3. Real-Life Example – From Data Scientist to Chief AI Officer

To understand how this transition works in practice, consider the story of **Shivani**, a data scientist who eventually became the **Chief AI Officer** of a leading technology firm. Shivani started as a machine learning engineer after completing her master's degree. She initially worked on a variety of machine learning projects, including predictive models for customer behavior and fraud detection.

However, Shivani always had a keen interest in the bigger picture—how AI could not just optimize individual processes but drive **entire business transformations**. After five years of deep technical experience, she sought out opportunities to evolve her role. She took on more responsibility by spearheading AI adoption strategies across different teams, collaborating with product managers to align AI initiatives with the company's vision.

In 2019, Shivani was promoted to **Director of AI Strategy**, and by 2021, she was named the **Chief AI Officer**. As CAIO, she now leads a team of data scientists, engineers, and AI researchers and works directly with the board of directors to drive the company's AI vision. Her journey from a technical role to a leadership position demonstrates that with a mix of technical expertise, strategic thinking, and leadership skills, you can climb the ranks to become an AI executive.

---

4. Quote: "The Journey of a Thousand Miles Begins with One Step." – Lao Tzu

As Lao Tzu's quote so beautifully captures, **every journey starts with a single step**. The transition from a beginner in AI to a seasoned practitioner, and eventually to a leader in the field, doesn't happen overnight. It takes time, effort, and perseverance.

You may feel overwhelmed by the sheer scale of the AI field, but every small step you take—whether it's learning a new algorithm, contributing to an open-source project, or leading a team—takes you closer to your ultimate goal. The key is to keep **moving forward**, one step at a time, with a vision of where you want to go.

AI is more than just a career; it's a **journey** of growth, discovery, and impact. By staying committed to lifelong learning, expanding your skills, and positioning yourself for leadership, you can achieve great things and help shape the future of AI.

Conclusion: Embrace the Journey

Growing your career in AI is not just about **mastering technical skills**; it's about positioning yourself for **leadership**, **influence**, and **long-term success**. The opportunities in AI are immense, and by staying updated with emerging trends, refining your skills, and evolving from a practitioner to a strategist, you can make a profound impact on the industry.

The road ahead will be challenging, but with every step, you will get closer to achieving your dreams. The future is waiting, and it's yours to shape.

References

1. Andrew Ng - "AI is the New Electricity"
   https://medium.com/machine-intelligence-report/andrew-ng-ai-is-the-new-electricity-21fca8449e1a
2. Coursera - AI and Machine Learning Online Courses
   https://www.coursera.org
3. Kaggle - Data Science and Machine Learning Competitions
   https://www.kaggle.com
4. GitHub - Contributing to Open Source AI Projects
   https://github.com
5. TensorFlow - Official Documentation and Resources
   https://www.tensorflow.org
6. PyTorch - Open-Source Machine Learning Framework
   https://pytorch.org
7. Jupyter Notebooks - Interactive Development Tool
   https://jupyter.org
8. Alan Kay - "The Best Way to Predict the Future is to Invent It"
   https://quoteinvestigator.com/2012/09/19/invent-the-future/
9. Benjamin Franklin - "An Investment in Knowledge Pays the Best Interest"
   https://founders.archives.gov/documents/Franklin/01-08-02-0055
10. Chris Grosser - "Opportunities Don't Happen. You Create Them"
    https://www.forbes.com/sites/forbescoachescouncil/2018/03/20/creating-opportunities-and-driving-career-success/
11. Jeff Bezos - "Your Brand is What Other People Say About You When You're Not in the Room"

https://www.inc.com/peter-roesler/jeff-bezos-top-10-quotes-on-entrepreneurship.html
12. Lao Tzu - "The Journey of a Thousand Miles Begins with One Step"
https://www.goodreads.com/quotes/71752-the-journey-of-a-thousand-miles-begins-with-one-step
13. AI Research Papers - arXiv
https://arxiv.org
14. NeurIPS (Conference on Neural Information Processing Systems)
https://nips.cc
15. Google AI Blog - Latest Updates and Innovations
https://ai.googleblog.com
16. Medium - AI and Machine Learning Articles
https://medium.com/tag/artificial-intelligence
17. OpenAI - Advancing AI for Humanity
https://openai.com
18. LinkedIn - Building Your Professional AI Brand
https://www.linkedin.com
19. EdX - Online Courses on AI and Data Science
https://www.edx.org
20. Udacity - AI Programming Nanodegree
https://www.udacity.com
21. ChatGPT - OpenAI's Conversational AI Tool
https://openai.com/chatgpt
22. DALL·E - AI for Generating Images from Text
https://openai.com/dall-e
23. MidJourney - AI-Based Art Creation Platform
https://www.midjourney.com
24. CVPR (Conference on Computer Vision and Pattern Recognition)
https://cvpr2024.thecvf.com

25. DataCamp - Online Training in Data Science and AI
    https://www.datacamp.com
26. Towards Data Science - AI Blog and Community
    https://towardsdatascience.com
27. Stack Overflow - Community for AI and Programming Questions
    https://stackoverflow.com
28. AI Ethics Resources - The Future of AI
    https://futureoflife.org/ai-safety/
29. AI Hackathons - List and Resources
    https://devpost.com/hackathons
30. MIT OpenCourseWare - Artificial Intelligence Courses
    https://ocw.mit.edu

Conclusion

As we reach the final chapter of this journey together, let's take a moment to reflect on the road we've travelled. From understanding the fundamentals of AI to exploring its vast career possibilities, building foundational skills, creating standout projects, and positioning yourself as a professional in the field, you've now been equipped with the tools, insights, and confidence to take the next step in your AI journey.

But let's be clear about one thing: **this is just the beginning.**

You've learned that AI isn't just a technology—it's a way of shaping the world. You've discovered how AI is already transforming industries, from healthcare to finance, and how your own career can contribute to that change. Along the way, we've met multiple people whose diverse stories reminded us that success in AI doesn't require you to start as an expert. It requires **curiosity, perseverance, and the courage to take the first step.**

We discussed the skills that matter—mathematics, programming, and domain knowledge. You now know where to start, whether you're a student aiming to build a foundation or a professional transitioning into this exciting field. The roadmap we outlined is more than a checklist; it's a guide to making AI a reality in your life.

The world of AI is **dynamic, fast-paced, and full of possibilities.** Today's tools and trends will evolve, but your ability to learn and adapt will ensure your relevance. Remember, AI is not about machines replacing humans; it's about **enhancing human potential.** The journey you're embarking on isn't about acquiring a single job—it's about building a career that will grow, adapt, and inspire.

You've started with knowledge, and now it's time to convert that knowledge into action. Take on new challenges, seek mentors, network with peers, and most importantly, build. Whether it's a project on Kaggle, an idea for an AI-driven solution, or simply contributing to an open-source initiative, each step forward will bring you closer to your goals.

In the end, the most important thing is your **belief in yourself.** AI is a vast field, and doubt may creep in—questions like, "Am I good enough?" or "Will I succeed?" Let me tell you, those doubts are normal. Everyone faces them, even the greatest pioneers of technology. What matters is how you respond.

As Franklin D. Roosevelt so wisely said, **"The only limit to our realization of tomorrow will be our doubts of today."** Let this quote guide you whenever self-doubt clouds your vision. Know that every effort you put in today will shape your tomorrow. Every course you take, every project you complete, every connection you build is an investment in a brighter future.

The field of AI is waiting for **your unique contribution.** The potential for impact is vast—solving real-world problems, improving lives, and creating a more innovative, connected world. Whether you dream of creating groundbreaking AI applications, leading digital transformations, or simply finding your place in this field, remember that you have the power to make it happen.

As you close this book, I hope it serves not as an end, but as a launchpad for your aspirations. The knowledge and stories shared here are meant to inspire you, guide you, and remind you that the future of AI isn't built by a few—it's built by people like you, bold enough to take the first step.

So, step forward with courage, curiosity, and commitment. Your AI journey begins now. The future belongs to those who dare to create it—**and that future includes you.**

This is your moment. Embrace it. Take that first step today and begin shaping a future not just for yourself, but for the world around you. Because in AI, as in life, the possibilities are endless—and so is your potential.

www.ingramcontent.com/pod-product-compliance
Lightning Source LLC
Chambersburg PA
CBHW071653240526
45469CB00023B/2287